# Suicide Bombers

## Elaine Landau

Twenty-First Century Books • Minneapolis

*For Michael*

Twenty-First Century Books
A division of Lerner Publishing Group
241 First Avenue North
Minneapolis, MN 55401 U.S.A.

Website address: www.lernerbooks.com


Library of Congress Cataloging-in-Publication Data

Landau, Elaine.
    Suicide bombers / by Elaine Landau.
        p.   cm.
    Includes bibliographical references and index.
    ISBN-13: 978–0–7613–3470–5 (lib. bdg. : alk. paper)
    ISBN-10: 0–7613–3470–X (lib. bdg. : alk. paper)
    1. Suicide bombers—Juvenile literature.  I. Title.
HV6431.L345  2007
363.325—dc22                              2005033422


Manufactured in the United States of America
1  2  3  4  5  6 – BP – 12  11  10  09  08  07

# TABLE OF CONTENTS

# A Note to the Reader

Dear Reader:

I am glad you have decided to read this book, but before I tell you what it is about, I would like to tell you what it is not about. This is not a book about how terrorism has affected our lives and the measures being taken to curtail it on an international level. Lots of good books covering that have already been written. It is also not a book about the impact of specific terrorist incidents. Unfortunately, there have been so many of these around the world that by the time you read about them in a book, newer ones have occurred. This book is also not about the key leaders of prominent international terrorist groups.

Instead, it is a close-up view of the foot soldiers of the terrorist movement—suicide bombers. It delves into the feelings and motivations of the young people who agree to blow themselves up for a cause. The text examines their backgrounds, families, and the societal and personal pressures that can make a sizable group of young people believe that killing themselves and others can ever be a solution.

Elaine Landau

On June 18, 2002, Mohammed al-Ghoul detonated a huge bomb packed with ball bearings and sharp nails inside a bus during the morning rush hour in south Jerusalem. Eighteen commuters and the bus driver died, and more than fifty were injured.

# SEEING BENEATH THE SURFACE

June 18, 2002 . . . The day started off much like any other for
Mohammed al-Ghoul, a twenty-two-year-old Palestinian
graduate student from the al-Farra refugee camp on the West
Bank. Early that morning, he said his prayers, ate breakfast,
and left his home ready to take on the day's activities.

Though Mohammed was from a fairly well-off Palestinian
family, he had lived in refugee camps most of his life due to
difficulties between the area's Jews and Arabs that began long
before his birth. He was one of the 700,000 Palestinians under
Israeli occupation. However, today Mohammed was leaving the
refugee camp for good. Instead of going to class at his
university, Mohammed was headed for Jerusalem. Once in
Jerusalem, he intended to detonate the explosives that he had
strapped to his waist and chest before leaving the house that
morning. If everything went according to plan, within hours
he would be dead.

It is hard to believe that the ordinary-looking young man in this photograph, a student known to be thoughtful and polite, is about to kill himself and nineteen others by choosing to become a suicide bomber.

It would take all of Mohammed's resolve to go through with the mission. The quiet student, known for his thoughtful and polite demeanor, was supposed to have carried out two previous suicide bombing missions, but both times he had lost his nerve and had not been able to go through with it. Now, in a suicide note later found by his parents, Mohammed wrote, "This time, I hope I will be able to do it."

Unfortunately, he managed to complete his mission that day. After arriving in Jerusalem, Mohammed boarded a bus packed with small children, students, and people commuting to work. He detonated the explosives, killing himself along with  nineteen other riders. Many more people were injured as well. Mohammed had been carrying an especially deadly bomb with him. Nails were embedded in the device to enhance its destructiveness. When the bomb exploded, these hot, sharp missiles shot through the air, piercing the terrified bus passengers.

In exploding the bomb, Mohammed al-Ghoul changed the way people would remember him forever. He would no longer be seen as a polite, studious young man. He was now a suicide bomber and would be thought of as a ruthless terrorist by some and a holy hero by others.

In some ways, suicide bombers have become the ultimate weapon of the poor. Besides causing death and destruction, they are extremely effective instruments of terror—no one

## TOO YOUNG TO DIE

Sixteen-year-old Iyad Marsi became extremely distraught when his fourteen-year-old brother was killed in an Israeli bombing raid in January 2004. Growing increasingly despondent and withdrawn, Iyad remained in his room most nights reading loudly from the Koran. Even after midnight, his family would hear him continuously playing taped Koran verses.

Iyad's parents thought that was just their son's way of dealing with the loss of his brother. They never dreamed that the teen had secretly met with members of the militant Palestinian group Islamic Jihad and arranged to become a suicide bomber. They would have stopped him if they had known. Yet as it turned out, Iyad Marsi did not get to go on his bombing mission after all. He died only days before when the explosive belt he had been given for the mission accidentally went off.

Now his parents are left to contend with the loss of two sons. Iyad's mother blames the radical Islamic organizations for taking advantage of young people who are upset and do not know how to effectively deal with their anger and grief. As Mrs. Marsi put it, "They [the militant groups] wash their brains [brainwash them] telling them about going to Paradise. These organizations incite them to be suicide bombers and teenagers aren't able to make such decisions."

knows when someone in a crowd might turn into a human bomb. Suicide bombers also help ensure the continued existence of the extremist groups that train and send them on missions. There is no chance of suicide bombers being caught and questioned because they always die with their victims and therefore cannot compromise others in the operation. To further add to their appeal to extremist groups, no sophisticated technology is needed to launch this devastating weapon. An extremist organization just has to have a supply of people who are ready and willing to blow themselves up.

Suicide bombers had become the weapon of choice for many of the Palestinian extremist groups taking part in the uprising against Israel known as the intifada. This was especially true after peace talks between the Israelis and Palestinians broke down in 2000. At that point, it did not look like the Palestinians would ever have their own state or get the Israelis to withdraw from the occupied territories.

Preferring death to a life without promise in a refugee camp, some Palestinians decided to retaliate. By sending suicide bombers into Israeli shops, restaurants, and nightclubs, militant Palestinian groups made sure the Israelis could not feel safe anywhere they were.

Since 2002, suicide bombers have played a dramatic role in the Palestinian struggle against Israel. These bombers are immediately elevated to hero status and become important symbols for such militant organizations as Hamas (meaning "Islamic Resistance" in Arabic), the Islamic Jihad (meaning "Holy Warriors" in Arabic), the Popular Front for the Liberation of Palestine (PFLP), and the al-Aqsa Martyrs Brigades.

Just hours following a suicide bomber's death, leaflets praising the bombing will frequently be heavily circulated throughout Palestinian refugee camps in the occupied

Two Palestinian youths walk past a wall covered with layers of posters, most of them glorifying the images of dead suicide bombers by portraying them as martyrs. Suicide bombers often pose for portraits in front of idyllic scenes before dying, perhaps to indicate the Paradise they believe awaits them.

territories. Often within days, an array of memorabilia honoring the bomber goes on sale. Suicide bombers are regarded by many as Palestinian martyrs who gave their lives in the name of Allah. In fact, as they strike, suicide bombers are told to cry out *"Allah Akhbar,"* or "God is great."

After the bombing, the religious aspect of the suicide bomber's actions is usually stressed. This is extremely important because Muslims are not permitted to commit suicide. However, they are allowed to give their lives to defend

# TROUBLE IN THE MIDDLE EAST

While tensions between Jews and Arabs in the Middle East date back to biblical times, the uneasy feelings reached a peak in 1947. At that time, the United Nations approved a plan to divide Palestine into two states—one to be Israel and the other Palestine. Unhappy with the creation of the new Jewish homeland, in 1948 a number of Arab nations attacked Israel. However, they were defeated, and as the victor, Israel took over some of the land that had been set aside for the Palestinians. As a result of the war, more than 700,000 Palestinians became refugees. The majority fled to Jordan including the West Bank, and the Gaza Strip, where they lived in crowded camps.

As time passed, the uneasiness between Israel and the Arab states continued to escalate, resulting in a number of armed struggles, which included the Suez War of 1956 and the Six-Day War of 1967. In the Six-Day War, Arab states had again joined forces to secure a victory against Israel, but instead they suffered a crushing defeat. This time, as a result of the war, Israel gained a good deal of territory, including control of the West Bank, the Gaza Strip, the Golan Heights, and all of Jerusalem.

Occupation of these areas by Israeli forces was especially hard for Palestinian refugees. There were accusations of excessive restrictions and Israeli brutality, and in 1987 the Palestinians in the West Bank and the Gaza Strip began an uprising against Israel known as the intifada. At various times, Israel's tactics in dealing with the Palestinian offenders included extensive jail sentences and demolishing their homes. After Israel was internationally criticized for using excessive force in dealing with the Palestinians in putting down this revolt, peace talks began and things calmed down somewhat.

To achieve peace, during the 1990s Israeli troops withdrew from parts of the Gaza Strip and the West Bank. However, in 2000 the peace process broke down, and the Palestinians began a second intifada. Palestinian suicide bombers struck throughout Israel and the occupied areas, killing hundreds of Israelis. Israel's forceful retaliation resulted in the death of many Palestinians and a reoccupation of portions of the West Bank. Key Palestinian leaders were also targeted for assassination. Though later on, Israel withdrew from some occupied areas, clashes between the two groups continued.

Finally in August 2005, Israel took the initiative for peace by beginning the first phase of a large-scale withdrawal of its settlers and troops from the region. Yet shortly after the removal of about 9,500 Israelis from settlements in the Gaza Strip and the West Bank, a suicide bombing took place outside a bus station in the southern Israeli city of Beersheba. Palestinian militants claimed that they had a right to retaliate for Israel's occupation crimes. Further tensions also arose between Israelis and Palestinians over Israel's plan to confiscate land around the West Bank settlement of Maaleh Adumin. The Israelis want this land to build a barrier separating Israel from Palestinian territory in order to secure their nation against further suicide bombings.

The hopes of many for achieving peace in the Middle East were dashed at the start of 2006. In the January 25 election, the militant group Hamas stunned the world by winning a majority of seats on the Palestinian Authority's legislative council. Hamas, which has called for the destruction of Israel, strongly supports the use of suicide bombers. The organization prides itself on being responsible for nearly half of the suicide bomber attacks against Israel between 2000 and 2005.

Following the election, world leaders urged Hamas to work for peace in the region. Although this remains an alternative, at this point, Hamas leaders have shown no inclination to do so. While campaigning for seats in the Palestinian government, Mahmoud Zahar, a top Hamas leader had actively emphasized the right of the Palestinian people to wage an armed struggle against Israel.

their faith, and liberating Muslims from Israeli control is seen as that. People who give their lives in defense of Islam (like suicide bombers) are considered martyrs. They are revered by some Palestinians as having attained the highest honor anyone can hope to achieve.

As explained by Dr. Abdul Aziz Rantisi, a pediatrician trained in Egypt who later became second in command of the political wing of Hamas in Gaza, "He who wants to kill himself because he's sick of being alive—that's suicide. But if someone wants to sacrifice his soul in order to defeat the enemy and for God's sake—well then he's a martyr."

These sentiments were echoed by the religious scholars at the Al-Azhar Center for Islamic Resistance, who published their own ruling on suicide attacks. It read, "When Muslims are attacked in their own homes and their land is robbed, the Jihad [holy war] for Allah turns into an individual duty, for men and for women equally. In those cases, operations of martyrdom become a primary obligation and Islam's highest form of Jihad."

Becoming a suicide bomber often brings a young person both fame and glory following his death. Numerous ceremonies and rallies are held to honor suicide bombers. Some are attended by large crowds of Palestinians who all chant the bomber's name and carry posters and banners bearing his picture.

When a successful mission involves a high number of Israeli fatalities, militant newspapers and magazines throughout the Middle East will frequently run stories and editorials praising the bomber and glorifying his actions. He becomes an instant idol to some in Palestinian communities. Schoolchildren will often carry postcard-sized pictures of the suicide bomber and claim that there is no one they admire more.

Palestinian children dressed like suicide bombers hold toy guns and slingshots during a rally in Gaza City, March 2001. The hooded children with fake explosives around their belts were put onstage to act out suicide attacks.

But are the actions of Palestinan suicide bombers really a desperate response to years of living in refugee camps? Do young people choose to become suicide bombers as an act of revenge against the perceived occupation of their rightful land by Israel?

Dr. Emanuel Savin, a terrorism expert, thinks so. He sees rage as the driving force behind most of the Palestinian suicide bombings. "It is the horrible situation under occupation," Savin noted. "Based on research I did in Algeria, I have to say that Israeli occupation is the major motivation for the Palestinians' readiness to commit suicide attacks."

## First Bombing under Hamas Rule

The first suicide bombing after Hamas took over the Palestinian government took place on April 17, 2006 during the Jewish holiday of Passover. Nine people were killed and 49 more were wounded when a bomb went off at a fast-food restaurant in a busy section of Tel Aviv, Israel. The suicide bomber was a Palestinian teenager named Sami Mohammed Hammed, who has been shown reading a statement in a video made prior to the bombing. In it, the teen dedicated the bombing to the Palestinian prisoners in Israeli jails and warned that many other bombers were on their way.

Yet some feel that the existence of suicide bombers raises some tricky questions. They wonder how seemingly typical young people can turn into killers overnight.

Are these individuals only striking out against Israel's treatment of their people, or are other factors involved? What really makes intelligent young people like Mohammed al-Ghoul choose to blow themselves up? According to Dr. Khaled Abou El Fadi, a distinguished jurist and scholar who has taught Islamic law at both Yale and Princeton, the motivations of suicide bombers are not always black and white. He feels that in some cases, becoming a suicide bomber may serve as an outlet for young people suffering from low self-esteem and feelings of inadequacy. As he noted in an interview:

> You are constantly reminded [as a Muslim youth] in everything—in the media, in school, on the radio, wherever you go—that we are a defeated culture, that we have lost our military battles, our economies have gone nowhere, our political institutions have gone nowhere and

so on. And this amazing sense of frustration makes you feel like, I've got to do something—do something. Well, here's where the easy way out [becoming a suicide bomber] comes in. . . . Someone comes in and says, now you're a hero; you can be a hero. You will be the talk of everyone. Everyone will remember you. People will put your pictures on walls, they'll put your face on walls and name factions after you—i.e. the martyrs of such and such. . . .

In further describing the possible allure of suicide bombing to young people, Dr. Khaled Abou El Fadi added,

So someone comes and poses as a scholar of Islamic law and says, "I can tell you that if you do this and do this, you have an immediate ticket to Heaven." . . . "You're going to be in a state of bliss." . . . Obviously, for very young kids, this starts sounding like, hey, it seems like all my problems are going to end in just one act, and if I can just marshal the bravery to do this one thing—take the anxiety, the fear, the pain that's going to go with this one act—all of my problems are solved forever.

Undoubtedly, the issue of suicide bombers demands further investigation. Only one thing is certain: there are no easy answers.

Israeli rescue forces examine a young shopper in the wreckage of the shoe store targeted by Wafa Idris.

# Chapter 2

# FEMALE SUICIDE BOMBERS

At first glance, twenty-seven-year-old Wafa Idris might have seemed like an ideal young woman. The soft-spoken Palestinian beauty was known to be intelligent as well as compassionate. Every Friday she worked as a volunteer with the Red Crescent Society ambulance crew to help save lives. Wafa was someone who comforted her widowed mother, doted on her nieces and nephews, and was liked and respected by those who worked alongside her.

Few could imagine that this poised, mild-mannered young woman, who enjoyed dressing chicly in Western-style clothing, would ever become a suicide bomber. Yet on January 27, 2002, she walked into an Israeli-owned shoe store in Jerusalem and, after examining the racks of stylish shoes, detonated a bomb that killed her and an eighty-one-year-old Israeli man and wounded more than one hundred others. That day the woman who had worked on the ambulance crew to save lives joined the ranks of the suicide bombers, becoming the first *shahida,* or female martyr.

"I don't understand it." That was what one of Wafa Idris's coworkers at the Red Crescent Society said after hearing that Wafa had blown herself up. "She [Wafa] was so happy when she was working. She was always so encouraging and optimistic to everyone she cared for. I never heard her say anything about violent retaliation or hate. It was only while we were waiting at the office for a call that she seemed depressed. Once she was looking through an old magazine and told me how she wished she could buy all the pretty clothes she wanted. But which one of us didn't want that?"

How does a young woman concerned about having enough pretty clothes to wear decide to become a suicide bomber? Those closest to Wafa knew of her dislike for the Israeli occupation, but they were also aware of some serious personal problems that seemed to crush Wafa's spirit.

The trouble began when Wafa was just a young girl and her father died, leaving the family without much money or other resources. Wafa's family decided that she should marry while she was still quite young. It was felt that this would make her more desirable since she would have many good childbearing years ahead of her. For Palestinian families living in refugee camps, having sons was among the most important things a woman could do, and her worth was determined accordingly. So in 1991, at just sixteen, Wafa married her cousin Ahmed, who conveniently lived in the same refugee camp.

Wafa was not upset about the arranged marriage as she had secretly had a crush on Ahmed for years. When she left her home to live with her husband and his parents, she dreamed of having a large family with the man she loved.

However, Wafa's future turned out not to be as bright as she had hoped. It took her over seven years to become pregnant, and then, to her horror, she gave birth to a stillborn baby girl. Wafa felt as though she had failed in her duties as a wife and that she was of no use to anyone. Though Ahmed loved Wafa, he was too overcome by the shame of being childless to be very supportive. His parents showed Wafa no pity, and even Ahmed felt the sting of the disgrace. He described his family's reaction: "At first my family blamed Wafa, and then they blamed me. They said that I was too weak to provide an infant that would survive in her womb."

Following the loss of her baby, Wafa became increasingly depressed. She refused to eat, stayed in bed for much of the day, and found it difficult to even carry on a conversation. At times, it seemed as if Wafa had lost the will to go on. Her best friend, Itimad Abu Lidbeh, saw it happening but felt as though Wafa was beyond her reach and did not know how to help her. "When she lost her baby, she lost her will to live," Wafa's friend explained. "I never understood why she reacted like that, but she did. She was a woman in enormous pain, and although she never said the words, I sensed that she had no desire to go on living."

Ahmed, Wafa's husband, was not terribly sophisticated and did not know what to do. The available medical assistance in the occupied territories was also not the best, and Wafa never got to see a fertility specialist or a psychiatrist. As the weeks passed, Wafa grew worse. Most days, she simply could not stop crying. When her husband saw that she was not improving, he decided to take a second wife, which, as a Muslim, he was permitted to do. But Wafa was still very much in love with her husband, and the thought of him taking another wife made her even more upset. When she refused to go along with the idea, Ahmed divorced her.

Wafa returned to her mother's house and within weeks watched Ahmed's wedding procession from her window as it joyously passed by. Wafa faced a good deal of humiliation following her divorce. Everyone in the refugee camp knew why her husband had divorced her. She was ridiculed and devalued as a woman unable to bear children.

Wafa no longer had anything to look forward to. She knew that in moving home, she was a financial burden to her family. She had no hope of ever remarrying, aware that no man in the camp would want a divorced woman who could not bear children. After a time, she decided that she would go back to Ahmed if he would have her. But by then, he and his new wife had two children and planned on having more. Ahmed was very happy with his new wife and when she insisted that Wafa not return, he agreed. That left Wafa

A series of personal disappointments moved Wafa Idris along the path toward becoming the first female suicide bomber, an act that led militant Palestinian organizations to realize that women and girls could be as effective as men and boys in bombing missions.

with a painful past to look back on and no future.

In some ways, Wafa had become a prisoner in a society that imposes many restrictions on women and offers them few choices or alternatives. Wafa knew that her family did not need an extra mouth to feed, but she had nowhere else to go. She may have felt boxed in and helpless, and when the militant Palestinian groups that sponsor suicide bombings felt they were ready for a woman suicide bomber, who had less to lose than Wafa Idris? Was it just a coincidence that she was chosen for this honor?

Suicide bombers are honored and respected, and there are also generous financial rewards for their families following their deaths. Often these families are given larger houses or apartments as well as substantial financial payments. The suicide bomber's family is also bathed in honor for having raised a young person noble enough for martyrdom. The memory of these martyrs lives on long after their death through songs and poems praising them. Often their pictures are plastered on buildings throughout the area where they lived, as an inspiration to others. If Wafa wanted to make up for the disgrace she had brought on her family as well as help them out of poverty, was there a better way? Furthermore, in her depression and confusion, was Wafa able to see any other way out?

The shame formerly experienced by Wafa's family as a result of her infertility and divorce was soon transformed into admiration. Suddenly, Wafa's childlessness became a choice as the young woman's history was quickly rewritten to fit her new image as a martyr. Wafa's aunt publicly proclaimed that Wafa had made a conscious decision not to have children because she wanted to be free to serve Allah and help her people. Speeches as well as newspaper articles heralded Wafa's

# A New Take on Women's Liberation

Some see the increasing number of women becoming suicide bombers as enlarging the societal role of women in Islamic nations. The following editorial, entitled "It's a Woman," appeared in the radical Egyptian newspaper *Al Sha'ab* in response to a suicide bombing mission carried out by a female. It read:

> It is a woman who teaches you today a lesson in heroism, who teaches you the meaning of Jihad and the way to die a martyr's death. It is a woman who has shocked the enemy, with her thin, meager, and weak body. . . . It is a woman who blew herself up, and with her exploded all the myths about women's weaknesses, submissiveness, and enslavement. . . . It is a woman who has now proven that the meaning of [women's] liberation is the liberation of the body from the trials and tribulations of the world . . . and the acceptance of death with a powerful, courageous, embrace.

However, many feminists would disagree with the sentiments expressed here. While they would like to see women achieve equality, they do not feel that women should have to blow themselves up to do so. They believe that true equality will come only when women are allowed to take their rightful place alongside men in government, the workplace, and society as a whole. Feminists further argue that having the courage to die for a cause is not a true measure of liberation. They stress that women have always been courageous but have just been limited in finding constructive ways to show it by the oppressive societies in which some live.

unselfish choice, giving her once tarnished reputation a golden new gleam.

Though Wafa Idris may have been the first female suicide bomber, she was certainly not the first suicide bomber to die for the Palestinian cause. Formerly, this role had been reserved for males. In Palestinian culture, women are expected to remain submissive to their fathers and brothers, who, in turn, protect them. For a woman to die for her people's cause while her father and brothers remain safely at home would have been a stain on a family's honor. However, this was not so in Wafa's case. Her actions had been carefully coordinated by an extremist group.

At first, extremist groups had frowned on women participating in any violent demonstrations. Islamic clerics (religious leaders) firmly stressed that women should remain in their traditional roles as wives and mothers. Yet in time, these cultural constraints began to break down. This was clearly evident in a speech given by former Palestinian leader Yasser Arafat on the morning of Wafa Idris's bombing mission. The then powerful Palestinian leader, who died in November 2004, told the crowd:

> Women and men are equal. You [women] are my army of roses that will crush Israeli tanks. You are the hope of Palestine. You will liberate your husbands, fathers, and sons from oppression. You will sacrifice the way you, women, have always sacrificed for your family.

Later that day, Wafa Idris became the first rose to die in Yasser Arafat's army of roses. Women, who may have feared that as suicide bombers they might be at odds with their faith, were assured by Sheik Yusuf al-Qaradawi, the influential fundamentalist cleric from Qatar, that this was not so. He issued a religious ruling stating that women "in Palestine" were eligible to join the other martyrs in Paradise.

Releasing women from the general constraints imposed on them by other clerics, he added that women on suicide bombing missions did not need to be accompanied by a chaperone to the attack site and could remove their veils if necessary. As the sheik explained, "She [the female suicide bomber] is going to die in the cause of Allah, and not to show off her beauty."

According to Yigal Carmon of the Middle East Media Research Institute, Sheik Yusuf al-Qaradawi's ruling is significant because many people needed a cleric of his stature to sanction the role of women as suicide bombers. "Everybody was not too comfortable with the whole thing, so it's important to have such a personality support it," Carmon noted.

The militant Palestinian organizations soon realized that they had found a valuable resource in utilizing female suicide bombers. They felt certain that at least initially the Israeli authorities would not be as likely to suspect females. Women were not as threatening as young males, and dressed in Western-style clothing—including jeans, short skirts, and modern hairstyles—Palestinian women easily blended in with the rest of the Israeli population.

Wafa Idris was just the first in what was to become a growing group of female suicide bombers. Some were highly educated professionals, whereas others were quite young and had little education. Yet a closer examination reveals that many were in the throes of a personal crisis at the time of their deaths.

Among these was a twenty-nine-year-old Palestinian woman named Hanadi Jaradat. Hanadi, who was unmarried and therefore childless, had left the West Bank for a time to attend law school in Jordan. She returned to her home in 1999 and began working at a local law office. In the United States, she might have been admired as a woman who had attained a great deal and who had a bright future ahead. However, among Palestinians, an unmarried twenty-nine-year-old woman was on the fringe of society.

Hanadi Jaradat's spirits plummeted when, in the spring of 2003, her brother Fadi along with her cousin were killed by Israeli forces. Hanadi reportedly stood over her brother's grave and swore to avenge his death. According to the Jordanian daily newspaper, *Al-Arab al-Yum,* she said, "Your blood will not have been shed in vain. The murderer will yet pay the price and we will not be the only ones who are crying." Weeping

Hanadi Jaradat blew herself up at an Arab-owned Haifa restaurant on October 4, 2003, killing twenty-one other people. Volunteers from the ultra-Orthodox Jewish rescue movement ZAKA are shown collecting body parts for proper Jewish burial.

bitterly, she added, "If our nation cannot realize its dream and the goals of the victims, and live in freedom and dignity, then let the whole world be erased."

While she was still in this highly emotional state, a female operative for the militant extremist group Islamic Jihad approached Hanadi. Recruiters for the group will frequently approach individuals struggling with grief and despair. At the time, they were also well aware of Hanadi's outsider status in their culture as an unmarried woman.

On October 4, 2003, about four months after the deaths of her brother and cousin, Hanadi Jaradat entered Maxim, a restaurant in Haifa, Israel, wearing enough explosives beneath her garments to blow up the building. It was midafternoon and the restaurant was packed with men, women, and children. A number of families had brought infants to the restaurant that day.

Hanadi detonated the bomb, killing herself along with twenty-one Israelis. Another forty-eight people were badly injured. The "Jerusalem Battalions," the military wing of the Islamic Jihad, took credit for the deed. They proclaimed Hanadi the "bride of Haifa," as female suicide bombers are believed to become the brides of Allah in Paradise. The group publicly stated that the "wedding in Haifa will teach the Zionists [Jews] an unforgettable lesson."

There have been other female suicide bombers as well. It is likely that being an unmarried woman was a factor in twenty-two-year-old Darin Abu Aisha's decision to become a suicide bomber. Known for her exceptional intellect, Darin was an outstanding student at the largest Palestinian university, Al-Najah University in Nablus. While Darin excelled in mathematics, she was even better at analyzing novels, poems, and plays and had decided to major in English literature. Darin had hoped to later continue her studies on a graduate level and one day teach at a university.

**Darin Abu Aisha actually searched for an Islamic extremist group that would use her as a human bomb. She was turned down by two, though the third provided her with explosives.**

A paper Darin had written for an essay contest at her school was so outstanding that the school printed and distributed it to other centers of learning throughout the Gaza Strip and the West Bank. She was even a guest on a local television show and became something of a celebrity on campus.

A number of young Palestinian men had wanted to marry Darin, but the youthful scholar was not interested. As her cousin Samira described the situation, "She refused them all. She was only interested in studying. Sometimes people teased her and called her names because she refused to marry and have children. Her parents suffered because of this."

Darin saw marriage and fulfilling the traditional role of the Palestinian woman as the end of her hopes and dreams. She wanted her academic achievements to open the door to a life filled with intellectual challenges in an environment where she could continue to learn and grow. She did not see how this could happen if she was pushed into an arranged marriage and expected to immediately bear children.

Though Darin hoped to remain single, her parents insisted that she do what was expected of her. Her best friend, Nano Abdul, felt that this might have been a factor in her decision to later become a suicide bomber. "There was enormous pressure on her to marry," Nano noted. "Her family was pleased with her academic achievements but they still felt that she was at university only until she married and had children. They were very upset when she announced that she had no intention of ever marrying because she had no intention of becoming a slave."

Though Darin desperately wanted her own life, she knew that by taking this path, she was subjecting her family to shame and ridicule, and that was something she had never wanted to do. Yet she hated the fate that awaited her. Perhaps Darin's sister Muna best expressed how Darin felt: "She [Darin] always said that in our society, human relationships were like a steel form into which we are poured by our family and which doesn't allow us to liberate ourselves from it and from the rules, dictated by tradition, which are so strict." Muna added that as the pressure on Darin to give up her dreams and conform continued, Darin became increasingly sad and bitter. She had even described her life as being "meaningless and insignificant."

However, a single unsettling incident in Darin's life may have helped bring her to her final decision to become a suicide bomber. It happened while Darin was waiting at a checkpoint set up by Israeli soldiers near Nablus. Darin was standing in line next to her cousin Rashid. Just behind them was a young mother holding an extremely ill infant. The mother begged the soldiers to let her pass through quickly as she had to get the baby to a hospital at once.

However, the soldiers refused to take the woman seriously. They insisted that she stop making a fuss and wait quietly in line until they had properly checked the documents of those ahead of her. Sensing that the baby might not have long to live, Darin tried to reason with the soldiers on the woman's behalf.

Still refusing to acknowledge the seriousness of the situation, the soldiers decided to have some fun at Darin's expense. They agreed to let the woman pass if Darin would allow the young man with her (her cousin Rashid) to kiss her on the mouth. Darin told the soldiers that it was a sin for a Muslim woman to kiss a man she was not married to. The soldiers either did not believe her or did not care, and to add to their fun, one of them even pulled Darin's *hijab* (head covering) off.

Darin was humiliated, but at that point, it looked as if the infant had stopped breathing and was beginning to turn blue. Hoping that by allowing Rashid to kiss her, she might save the child's life, she told him to do it. Though it shocked the other Muslims in line, at least the soldiers kept their word and allowed the woman with the ill infant to pass.

The following day, Rashid arrived at Darin's home to ask her to marry him. Under the circumstances, Darin now had to marry Rashid to save her honor and that of her family. By then, everyone in the camp had heard what happened and it was doubtful that any other Muslim man would ever want Darin as his bride.

While Darin's parents were anxious for the wedding to take place, Darin wanted no part of it. Her feelings about marriage had not changed and though she was fond of her cousin, she did not see him as her life partner. As a pious Muslim who firmly believed in her faith, Darin found her own way out of this predicament. She would save her parents from being publicly shamed and at the same time strike a blow against Israeli occupation. Darin Abu Aisha became a suicide bomber.

On February 27, 2002, she blew herself up at the Maccabim checkpoint near Jerusalem. Just before the explosion, she called her mother to apologize for sneaking out of the house that day. Then Darin did what she set out to do. In seconds, a young life that had held so much promise was over. Darin's body and future were blown to pieces.

Female suicide bombers have also made their presence felt in Iraq. As early as April 4, 2003, two women carried out a suicide car bomb attack against U.S. and coalition forces based there. Three coalition soldiers were killed while two civilians were badly wounded. Following the bombing, a videotape of the two women was shown on the Qatar-based Al Jazeera network. On the videotape, the women were seen holding a Koran and a machine gun. Some reports indicate that one of the women was pregnant at the time of the attack.

More recently, an attack involving a female suicide bomber occurred on September 28, 2005, in Tal Afar, Iraq, near the Syrian border. There, a young woman wearing a male's robe and headdress to disguise herself as a man managed to slip into a line of Iraqi army recruits. The recruits were seen as cooperating with the invading American and British forces and therefore considered a suitable target. While in line, she detonated the explosives strapped to her body with deadly consequences. At least six of the men in line with her were killed and more than thirty-five others wounded in the explosion. The woman, who appeared to be in her early twenties, was identified only as a "blessed sister" by al-Qaeda of Iraq—the militant group claiming responsibility for the attack.

Earlier in March 2005, four female suicide bombers wearing explosive belts were stopped in a town south of Baghdad before they could detonate their bombs. Some feel that these events are a sign of a growing number of women willing to become suicide bombers. Major General Hussein Ali Kamal, head of intelligence at the Iraqi Interior Ministry, feels that the Tal Afar attack "rings danger alarms." Indeed, suicide bombing may be on its way to becoming "an equal opportunity" way to die.

# Chapter 3
## CHARACTERISTICS
## OF SUICIDE BOMBERS

Hussam Abdo is a fifteen-year-old boy who nearly became a suicide bomber. Outfitted with a belt of explosives strapped to his body, he was headed for his target when Israeli forces stopped him. Following his arrest, Hussam was interviewed by the British Broadcasting Company (BBC) for a documentary on suicide bombers. The following is an excerpt from that interview:

> **Interviewer:** What is the main reason for your deciding to become a suicide bomber? The one reason in particular.
> **Hussam:** The reason was because my friend was killed. The second reason I did it was because I didn't want to go to school. My parents forced me to go to school and I didn't feel like going.
> **Interviewer:** It seems extreme that if you don't like your teacher it could partially propel you towards murder and suicide.

**Hussam:** The thing is my parents forced me to go to school and I didn't want to go.

Few people would say that Hussam is a typical suicide bomber, but if the Israelis had not detected him, he would have joined the growing list of martyrs. So if Hussam is not the average suicide bomber, who is?

Some Israeli secret service analysts feel that today there may actually be no "typical suicide assassin." Early on, when the first wave of suicide bombings began in the 1990s, most of the human bombers tended to be young males who were poor and ultrareligious. Brigadier General Nizar Ammar of the Palestinian General Security Organization would agree; he listed the characteristics of the typical suicide bomber at that time as follows:

> Young, often a teenager.
> He is mentally immature.
> There is pressure on him to work.
> He can't find a job.
> He has no options, and there is no social safety net to help him. . . .
> He has no girlfriend or fiancée. . . .
> No means for him to enjoy life in any way.
> Life has no meaning but pain.
> Marriage is not an option—it's expensive and he can't even take care of his own family.
> He feels he has lost everything.
> The only way out is to find refuge in God.
> He goes to the local mosque. . . .
> He begins going to the mosque five times a day—even for 4 A.M. prayers. . . .

However, this profile no longer fits suicide bombers. Now there are female suicide bombers, and today some suicide bombers come from well-off families. And, of course, there's also Hussam, whose main motivation for becoming a suicide bomber appeared to be not wanting to go to school.

It has been argued that at times suicide bombers act out of a sense of despair while living under Israeli occupation. As Labib Kamhawi, a Jordanian political analyst put it, "What prompts a twenty-year-old to blow himself up and kill as many Israelis as he can in the process? It definitely takes more than belief in God to turn a boy into a martyr. It takes desperation, anger, and loss of hope. It's believing that your life is not worth living anymore."

Dr. Eyad Sarraj, founder and director of the Gaza Community Mental Health Programme, underscored these sentiments in a commentary published in August 2001 entitled, "Why We Have Become Suicide Bombers." Sarraj wrote:

> Israeli occupation means that you are called twice a year by the [Israeli] intelligence for routine interrogation and persuasion to work as an informer on your brothers and sisters. No one is spared. If you are known to be a member of a political organization, you will be sentenced to ten years. For a military action, you will be sentenced to life.
>
> To survive under Israeli occupation, you are given the chance to work in jobs that Israelis do not like: sweeping the streets, building houses, collecting fruit or harvesting. You will have to leave your home in the refugee camp in Gaza at 3 A.M., go through the road blocks and check posts, spend your day under the sun and surveillance, returning home in the evening to collapse in bed for a few hours

before the following day. We simply became slaves of our enemy. . . . The amazing thing is not the occurrence of the suicide bombing but rather the rarity of them.

The same reasoning could be applied to the suicide bombers in Iraq in response to the American military presence there following the overthrow of Saddam Hussein. In an interview with an Iraqi suicide bomber "in training" (using the pseudonym "Marwan Abu Ubeida" to protect his identity), American journalists were given a glimpse of what may be motivating some suicide bombers.

Marwan had led a privileged life in Fallujah when Saddam Hussein was president of Iraq. As a successful businessman, his father had made more than enough to support Marwan along with his ten other children. Though Fallujah had been an important power base of support for Saddam, unlike many others there, Marwan was not upset over the dictator's fall. Instead he was enraged over the American occupation following Saddam's overthrow. As he put it, "We expected them [the Americans] to bring Saddam down and then leave but they stayed and stayed."

Marwan, along with one of his older brothers, was among those who joined the resistance against the Americans. In April 2003, in retaliation for American soldiers' firing into a crowd of demonstrators, Marwan and a few others gathered grenades from an abandoned Iraqi army site and threw them at a building where there were U.S. soldiers. "They [the U.S. soldiers] shot back but couldn't hit any of us," Marwan reported in describing the incident. "It was my first taste of victory against the Americans."

Over the next year, Marwan was involved in at least twelve more such incidents. In time, he became quite proficient with a machine gun, which brought him to the attention of some of the leaders of a broad-scale insurgent group known as Attawhid wal Jihad. As Marwan was also a devout Muslim who took his Koran studies at his local mosque seriously, these men were impressed with his strict religious devotion.

When they later suggested that he become a suicide bomber, Marwan felt honored. Like most Iraqis who take on this role, Marwan has severed ties with his family, though he claims that he will call them to say good-bye just prior to his mission. While others in Marwan's family are active in the resistance to American occupation, they feel that Marwan has gone too far in agreeing to become a suicide bomber.

Nevertheless, at this point in his life, Marwan would prefer to be around the jihadists (fighters in a holy war) in any case. "The jihadists are more religious people," he said in describing them. "You ask them anything—anything—and they can instantly quote a relevant section from the Koran. . . . My family is not happy with my choice," Marwan admits. "But they know they can't change my path."

Ideally, Marwan would like a strict Islamic fundamentalist regime to take over in Iraq, but he does not expect to live long enough to see that. He explained, "The first step is to remove

## FACTS ABOUT SUICIDE BOMBERS

- 47 percent of suicide bombers have a college education, and an additional 29 percent are at least high school graduates.
- 83 percent of all suicide bombers are unmarried at the time of the attack.
- 64 percent of suicide bombers are between 18 and 23 years old; in some cases, suicide bombers have been even younger.
- 68 percent of suicide bombers have come from the Gaza Strip.

the Americans from Iraq. After we have achieved this, we can work out the other details." Though Marwan uses the word "we," it is clear that he knows that he will not be among those working out the details.

According to U.S. Navy Commander Fred Gaghan, head of the Combined Explosives Exploitation Cell in Iraq, young people like Marwan are not a rarity. Gaghan's unit has investigated a large number of suicide bombings, and they have continued to occur. As for finding recruits for what many Americans would regard as a grisly task, the commander noted

The image of the suicide bomber as a hero and a martyr was certainly being propagated in Iraq during the reign of Saddam Hussein. Iraqi boys are shown dressed as suicide bombers marching in a parade to celebrate their leader's sixty-fifth birthday in 2002.

that "they [the insurgent leaders] have plenty of volunteers who will do it willingly."

Apparently, many of these volunteers come to Iraq from other countries. American authorities in Iraq report that young would-be suicide bombers from Syria, Yemen, and especially Saudi Arabia have streamed into Baghdad to join the infamous terrorist leader Abu Musab al-Zarqawi in a holy war against the American occupiers. Many of these youthful volunteers are teenagers or in their early twenties, and a large number of them have grown up in comfortable middle-class homes. As one jihadist described them, "They have got no experience, they are not trained. They just have to drive the vehicle [for a car bomb]. But these boys—17, 18 years old are important [to the struggle]." When asked about their motivation, the jihadist replied, "I think their religion is [a] better [reason] than others. They are rich, they are educated, and they need nothing, but they see that in this fight they will win either victory or heaven. This is their ideology. Either way, they win."

Similar claims have come from leaders in the Palestinian fight against Israel. According to one unnamed Hamas recruiter, "The selection process [for suicide bombers] is complicated by so many people wanting to be taken on this journey of honor! If we choose one, countless others are disappointed. They have to learn to be patient and wait until God calls them. [The dilemma facing the militant Palestinian groups is that there] are the hoards of young men who come banging on our door, begging us to send them on a mission. It's difficult to choose just a few of these. The ones we send away just keep coming back, badgering us, begging us, beseeching us to accept them for a mission."

As suicide is strictly forbidden for Muslims, those organizing suicide-bombing missions go to a great deal of trouble to continually stress that the suicide bombers are soldiers or jihadists in a holy war. Often the term *holy warrior* will be used in referring to suicide bombers, and the bombing itself is termed a *holy explosion.* Yet suicide bombers are not trained in the same way other warriors or soldiers are. Though most soldiers may be willing to risk their safety for their country, they are trained to survive, while suicide bombers are trained to accept their own death while taking others with them.

Despite the insistence by some militant extremist groups that suicide bombers are not committing suicide, in her book, *Terror in the Name of God: Why Religious Militants Kill,* U.S. terrorism expert and Harvard University lecturer Jessica Stern points out that there are some striking similarities between ordinary suicide and suicide bombings.

"Ordinary suicide has been shown to spread through social contagion, especially among youth," asserts Stern. "Studies have shown that a teenager whose friend or relative attempts or commits suicide is more likely to attempt or commit suicide himself. . . . The situation in Gaza suggests that suicide-murder can also be spread through social contagion, that at some tipping point a cult of suicide-murder takes place among youth. Once this happens, the role of the organization appears to be less critical; the bombing takes on a momentum of its own. 'Martyrdom operations' have become part of the popular culture in Gaza and the West Bank."

The myth and adoration surrounding suicide bombers are hard to miss in these regions. Instead of putting on a play as children elsewhere might do, children in Gaza often stage mock funerals for the latest suicide bombers. Furthermore, if you walked into a classroom filled with Palestinian children and asked them to list the heroes they most admire, it is

At a 2005 rally celebrating the Israeli withdrawal from the Gaza strip, a young Palestinian boy displays his political orientation in the form of a T-shirt with a picture of the late president Yasser Arafat on it and a fake suicide bomb belt around his waist.

highly likely that a number of suicide bombers will be mentioned.

Since most suicide bombers are young, many young people tend to readily identify with them and long for the glory lavished on these "holy warriors." This may help to explain the large numbers of young volunteers for suicide bombing missions that extremist group leaders boast of.

In some cases, becoming a martyr may have special appeal for adolescent boys. The organizations that send them on these missions often stress that the martyr's reward in Paradise is his marriage to seventy-two black-eyed virgins. Living in a society where devout Muslims do not have sex before marriage or even kiss a girl for that matter, the thought of this reward can be especially enticing. As a sixteen-year-old youth who is active in Hamas put it, "I know that my life is poor compared to Europe and America but I have something awaiting me that makes all my suffering worthwhile. . . . Most boys can't stop thinking about the virgins." One of the young would-be suicide bombers stopped by Israeli authorities was found to have carefully wrapped layers of toilet paper around his genitals. Supposedly, he had hoped to shield this part of his body for future use in Paradise.

The varied characteristics and possible motivations of suicide bombers have led researchers to take a more in-depth look at these individuals. While some may have been depressed, confused, or felt boxed in by societal restrictions at the time of the suicide attack, psychologists have not found suicide bombers to be deranged psychopaths on the loose. Todd Stewart, a retired Air Force general who now directs the Program for International and Homeland Security at Ohio State University, noted, "There is little to no evidence that they [suicide bombers] are mentally unbalanced." Stewart further said that these individuals are "not necessarily from fanatically religious families."

Anthropologist Scott Attran, a research director at the National Center for Scientific Research in Paris, France, received funding from the National Science Foundation to interview would-be suicide bombers in Gaza and the West Bank. In reporting on his findings, Dr. Attran stated, "None of the supporters of suicide terrorism I interviewed, especially at Al-Najah University, were poor, uneducated, socially estranged or psychologically deranged. They are idealistic and compassionate, and think they can change the world. That makes the whole thing more frightening than if they were just crazies off the street." Forensic psychiatrist Marc Sageman, of the University of Pennsylvania, found a similar pattern through his research. In describing this group, Sageman said that many would-be suicide bombers attended college, were economically well off, and were often "the elite of their countries."

Yet despite the differences among suicide bombers and the many misconceptions about them, there is one thing that is common to the vast majority of these individuals. Suicide bombers do not act on their own. There is almost always an organization behind them. The organization recruits and trains those slated to go on suicide missions. It determines the time, the place, and the target and is vital to the suicide bomber's success.

## OF DIFFERENT MINDS

The vast majority of Muslim religious leaders are against suicide bombings, insisting that these actions violate the basic principles of Islam. They stress that the Prophet Muhammad strictly forbade harming innocent bystanders, even during wartime. Even radical Islamic clerics who see suicide bombers as defenders of the faith differ in how they believe these operations should be carried out. Mohammed Sayed Tantawi, a leading authority on Islam, noted the following in Egypt's *Al Ahram* newspaper: " . . . if a person blows himself up, as in operations that Palestinian youths carry out against those they are fighting [soldiers], then he is a martyr. But if he explodes himself among babies or women or old people who are not fighting the war, then he is not considered a martyr."

Yet, on the other hand, Egyptian cleric Sheik Yusuf al-Qaradawi is quoted in the Qatari newspaper *Al Raya* as saying, "They are not suicide operations. They are heroic martyrdom operations, and the heroes who carry them out don't embark on this action out of hopelessness and despair but are driven by an overwhelming desire to cast terror and fear into the hearts of the oppressors."

Many people currently believe that understanding the group's motivation and operation is the key to understanding suicide bombings. Todd Stewart is among those who feel that we need to study group dynamics rather than individual psychology to best understand what leads a person to use his or her body as a weapon. As he put it, "Group norms [values and goals] are more important than individual traits" when it comes to creating a suicide bomber. Perhaps organizational masterminds are more vital to the success of this terrorist tactic than the human bombers themselves are.

# Chapter 4

# RECRUITERS AND TRAINERS

At first glance, suicide bombers may appear to work alone. Once the deed is done, there's no one left for authorities to question. Yet what might seem like a quick and simple act often involves months of careful planning on the part of an extremist organization. According to Dr. Ariel Merari, an Israeli political violence expert, every suicide bombing involves a minimum of ten people. For security purposes, each person knows only the direct contact above him or her. The identities of the others in on the plan are kept secret. That way, if anyone is discovered, the entire team is not jeopardized. As Dr. Merari put it, "[Suicide bombing missions are always] highly secretive. Each person or link has a specific job, and knowledge is imparted on a need to know basis."

Despite the praise lavished on suicide bombers by their recruiters and trainers, the individuals sent out to die are never key leaders or major figures in an extremist organization.

Instead, a suicide bomber is viewed as a dispensable person. In the words of a trainer who guides these individuals on their missions, "The . . . people who commit acts of martyrdom are not *stars* in the organization. They are people seeking revenge for acts done against us."

On the whole, suicide bombers tend to be fairly young, while the organization leaders are often more mature and politically savvy. It might be argued that extremist organizations cannot afford to blow up their top people because the group needs their leadership ability and strategizing skills. Yet interestingly, the children of the movement's leaders rarely become suicide bombers either. Often these children are sent far from the "battle zone" areas where danger and deprivation characterize everyday life. Instead, many attend exclusive private schools in Amman, Jordan, Europe, and elsewhere. When Palestinian Liberation Organization (PLO) leader Yasser Arafat was alive, his wife and daughter were sent to live in luxurious accommodations in Paris. In addition, in March 2002, a number of witnesses swore that the first thing one of Arafat's military leaders said to his lawyer when he was arrested by the Israelis was, "Tell my wife to watch our sons and daughters so they don't go off on a suicide operation."

Those who recruit and train the bombers also do not volunteer to blow themselves up. When one trainer was asked by an interviewer if he would ever consider becoming a suicide bomber, his answer was a firm "no." "This is an organization," the young man was quick to explain." Every person has his own role." When further asked if he ever felt any remorse over the young people who are lost on these one-way missions, his answer again was no. "The terrible things that have happened to the Palestinian people are far bigger and far stronger than feeling sorry or guilty. As a Palestinian, I feel that my people have been murdered." Clearly, he had no difficulty turning other young Palestinians into human grenades for revenge.

The field operatives who train suicide bombers spend a good deal of time determining how such operations can best benefit their cause. From their viewpoint, the worst thing that can happen is having the bomber detected by Israeli authorities prior to completing the mission. Therefore, a great deal of time and energy goes into disguising these human bombers. Dressed as Israelis, suicide bombers are nearly impossible to pick out in a crowd. Yet one Palestinian extremist leader, who went by the name Warden, noted that disguises are not always enough: "Around ten operations failed because the men weren't walking properly," he explained. "They were too quick, too anxious; they were in too much of a hurry. Apart from that, their disguise was perfect: some were wearing army uniforms; others were clean-shaven; others wore earrings or wigs or the gear of the ultra-Orthodox [Jews]. But no one dressed like that would normally rush around nervously."

Other times, would-be suicide bombers have changed their minds at the last minute, thwarting the plans of field operatives. This once happened to Ibrahim Sarahne, who helped implement suicide bombings for the group al-Aqsa Martyrs Brigades. Ibrahim Sarahne was quite an asset to the extremist al-Aqsa Martyrs Brigades before his arrest by Israeli authorities in June 2002. Sarahne was a Palestinian living in the Dehaishe refugee camp who had gone through all the necessary scrutiny to obtain the papers needed to drive a taxicab on Israeli streets.

This permitted him to easily pass through Israeli

checkpoints—something that other operatives in extremist organizations often had trouble doing. The al-Aqusa Martyrs Brigades leaders immediately saw how Sarahne could be instrumental to them in facilitating suicide bombings. He would be able to carry the bombers across the Israeli border in his taxi. Then they could travel anywhere in Israel without being subjected to scrutiny.

Though not a devout Muslim, Sarahne was eager to assist the extremist group as he deeply resented the Israelis for their treatment of his people. "God played no part in my decision," Sarahne noted in describing his motivation. "This was about pure force, I don't like to be pushed around."

Having Sarahne's help gave the al-Aqusa Martyrs Brigades an added benefit as well. Sarahne knew Israel's streets and was well aware of which areas were especially crowded at different times of the day. This was crucial in determining where a suicide bomber could have the greatest impact. Sarahne was extremely proud of his effectiveness and even boasted about it.

"I took my job very seriously and I was always careful," he noted. "I was able to get away with it because the authorities never suspected me. I had the right identification and I understood the Israeli mentality. After all, I listened to so many Israelis in the backseat of my cab who claimed to like good Palestinians, the ones who were grateful for the crumbs and who didn't rebel or make trouble. . . . But after I dropped off a bomber and heard the ambulances and sirens [from a distance] and knew it had gone off as planned, partly because of me, I can't describe the feeling of pure joy that I felt in my heart."

Of course, not every attempt was successful. On May 22, 2002, Sarahne was driving two suicide bombers to their target when things did not go quite according to plan. The suicide

bombers he was escorting that day were extremely young—
one was a fourteen-year-old boy called Mahmoud, and the
other was a sixteen-year-old girl named Arin Ahmed. Arin
agreed to become a suicide bomber after Israeli soldiers
supposedly killed her boyfriend. Eager for justice, Arin was
determined to avenge his death and "follow him to Paradise."
Only later did she learn that her boyfriend was actually killed
when a bomb he was transporting accidentally exploded. No
Israelis were anywhere near at the time.

In any case, the goal of the double suicide bombing that
evening was to kill as many Israelis as possible. Mahmoud was
to blow himself up first. Once all the emergency personnel had
arrived, Arin would detonate herself. That way the emergency
crews would be killed, the injured could not get help, and even
more people would die.

Yet as Sarahne was driving the teen bombers to the site, the
pair began to have second thoughts. Arin said that when she
saw the women and children in the crowd, she knew that she
could not go through with it. "I thought there were only going
to be soldiers," she would later explain.

Sarahne tried to talk both teens into going through with it.
His wife, who had come along on the mission and was also
actively involved in helping to stage the suicide attacks, was
persuasive too. While Mahmoud broke down and agreed to do
as he had promised, Arin still refused. So after Mahmoud blew
himself up, taking fifteen Israelis to the grave with him,
Sarahne, his wife, and Arin headed home.

If becoming a suicide bomber is truly a voluntary act and
there really is a flood of volunteers for these missions, we'll
never know why Sarahne's wife behaved as she did on the ride
back. As Arin described it, "All the way back in the car, Irena
[Sarahne's wife] kept yelling at me and pulled my hair. She

spat on me and called me a brat, a coward, a baby, and a disgrace to all Palestinian women. . . . She was crazed." Yet Ibrahim Sarahne was not discouraged. He was pleased with Mahmoud's decision and claimed, "the operation was [a] success."

That incident notwithstanding, after a while, the people who select and train suicide bombers tend to develop an intuitiveness or "sixth sense" about which individuals will go through with these deadly missions. Their chief recruiting areas for suicide bombers are mosques and universities. Many young people join extremist organizations when they go to universities because their friends join, and it just seems like the right thing to do. At least at first, most of these youths are not particularly religious or political. Such young people generally will not volunteer for a suicide mission and are not approached.

Instead, those selected are often young, unattached males who are extremely religious and well thought of at their mosques. As a rule, young men who are the sole breadwinners for their families will not be taken. The same generally holds true for only sons. Other deeply religious young males, however, may be prime targets. Psychologist Ariel Merari believes that the most important characteristic of those chosen for these missions is their susceptibility to the group's propaganda. This is crucial in ensuring that the suicide bomber is thoroughly committed to the task at hand.

Once an individual agrees to become a suicide bomber, a period of intense indoctrination begins. This is the bomber's training time, and during it, much of what he or she does will be orchestrated by the assigned trainer.

First, the would-be suicide bomber starts a program to cleanse his or her mind and soul as well as help him or her attain the personal discipline necessary to carry out the task ahead. One suicide-bomber-in-training from Iraq described what he had to do this way: "Besides the Koran, I read about the history of jihad, about great martyrs who have gone before me. These things strengthened my will."

A martyr-in-training will usually spend much of the day listening to tapes that tell of the many rewards awaiting him or her in heaven. These tapes describe an ideal life after death, one far more glorious than anything that young person ever experienced on Earth. In their book, *The Road to Martyrs' Square: A Journey Into the World of the Suicide Bomber,* authors Anne Marie Oliver and Paul Steinberg assert that many would-be suicide bombers are told some version of the following:

> Awakening not on earth but rather in the Gardens of Delight, the martyr would find himself surrounded by all good things. Rather than the rivers of sewerage that ran through the camp where he was born, there would be rivers of milk and honey and wine. He would lie on luxurious couches beneath beautiful trees, feeling neither heat nor cold, pain nor sorrow. Seventy-two beautiful women . . . would be his for the taking. . . . "

During this indoctrination time, the would-be suicide bomber would also listen to tapes that tell stories of fearless jihadists fighting the Russians in Afghanistan years earlier to defend Islam. Some jihadist groups also like to show the bombers-in-training videotaped suicide bombings that inflicted sizable Israeli casualties.

Frequently, after joining a militant extremist group, would-be suicide bombers begin to mentally and emotionally withdraw from their families. The intense indoctrination makes them begin to feel closer to their trainer and the other jihadists who believe in the same course of action. One suicide bomber summed up this tendency when he said, "You give up your previous life and start a new one."

During this new life, the would-be suicide bomber is often referred to as a living martyr. He'll make audio tapes and videotapes to be used following the bombing as a farewell statement to inspire others. Bombers-in-training will also leave an array of impressive photos in which they have been told to strike a heroic pose. These will later be used for recruitment posters and calendars. These steps have the added benefit of further bonding the individual to the group and its overall aims and goals. With each step forward, it becomes increasingly difficult for the young person to experience a change of heart and contemplate backing out. It would certainly be hard for any young person to trade honor and adoration for the humiliation of being seen as a coward who changed his or her mind. Instead, most bombers-in-training see their fate as sealed and go along with the program.

Interestingly, in the last weeks before their deaths, suicide bombers often appear euphoric. Those who have interviewed suicide bombers shortly before their missions have frequently noted this elation. As the authors of the *Road to Martyrs' Square* noted,

> These guys know they are going to die. . . . At the same time, we get the feeling that life has never seemed better to them—so intense, so exuberant, so full of meaning. Perhaps that's why they just keep smiling—They just can't believe that they're about to become Martyrs, about to take

This portrait of Maher Hebeishi—who blew himself up in Haifa in December 2001, killing fifteen people and injuring forty others—was released by his family after his death. It shows him dressed as a Muslim pilgrim in front of a backdrop of the holy Muslim city of Mecca.

their place in the roster of great men. Who would ever have believed it? They must be thinking. . . . They've never gotten so much attention in their lives. . . ."

One Iraqi suicide bomber in training had a close friend who blew himself up at a checkpoint set up by American soldiers. Prior to his friend's going off on his mission, the two young men had "made a pact" to "meet in heaven." The bomber-in-training had also noticed that his friend seemed jubilant prior to his death. "My friend was happier than I had ever seen him. He felt he was close to the end of his journey to heaven," the bomber trainee explained. At that point, would-be suicide bombers fully believe what their trainers have taught them about going to "the happy death" reserved for martyrs. By then they have taken to heart such organization slogans as:

> *I will die someday in order that my religion live.*
> *Oh Muslims, say "Allah Akhbar" with joy, and let's march forward carrying our coffins.*
> *How sweet is death for the sake of the homeland.*
> *What is more beautiful than to die alone in order that a million might live.*
> *Mother, I am happy, happy to die for freedom.*

The trainer helps to remove any remaining fear of death that the would-be suicide bomber has by having that individual repeatedly picture his or her death under glorious circumstances. In fact, these individuals are taught to avoid dying of natural causes at all costs. As PFLP operatives like to say, "Beware of natural death. Don't die except in a shower of bullets."

When asked if they feel badly about the pain their parents will experience as a result of their death, suicide bombers refuse to take responsibility for their choices. They believe their trainers, who insist that Allah chooses all suicide bombers. They are merely answering his call.

The trainers also stress that they have Allah's blessings in killing Israelis as well as American soldiers in Iraq. Both are seen as non-Muslim invaders in a Muslim land. Therefore, the suicide bombers are defending their faith when they go on these missions.

As one trainer noted:

> Everyone in Israel is a fair target. They are all occupying Palestinian land. . . . We as a Muslim race are against the killing of women and older people. But I'd like to make one thing clear. Anyone who occupies one piece of land in Palestine is worthy of being killed by us. We have the right to kill anyone who occupies our land. We believe in an eye for an eye and a tooth for a tooth. He who begins the aggression is the unjust one. When the Jews return to their original country, where they came from, America, Poland, or any other place in Europe, then maybe we will consider they are forgiven and we will not kill them anymore. But as long as they are in our country, we have a right to kill them.

In training, suicide bombers are also taught to dehumanize their victims so it is easier to kill them. Jerald Post, a psychologist at George Washington University in Washington, DC, found this through interviewing thirty-five Palestinian terrorists who had been captured and imprisoned. After speaking with them, he learned that suicide bombers are taught to see their victims as the enemy. Even small children are not viewed as young and innocent but as people who will someday grow up to be the enemy.

Although an organization's field commander, along with the explosives experts and others in the group, determine the time

## Pride in a Deadly Job

Some Iraqi suicide bombing coordinators are so highly skilled that their services are sought out by a number of insurgent groups. That is the case with Al-Tamimi (not his real name) who has helped coordinate over thirty suicide bombing missions in Iraq. Al-Tamimi is likely to be the last person the suicide bomber sees before completing his mission. As he described his role in the training process, "Once a volunteer is placed in my care, I am responsible for everything in his life until the time comes for him to end it."

Al-Tamimi serves as the suicide bomber's guide and guardian. He especially likes working with the foreign recruits who come to Iraq to carry out suicide bombings, as he feels these individuals are the most enthusiastic about what they hope to achieve. He describes the suicide bomber he is currently working with as a Saudi who is barely past his teens. "You can't imagine how excited and happy he is," Al-Tamimi said of the youth. "He can't stop smiling and laughing, even singing. He is sure he is going to Paradise, and he just can't wait."

Al-Tamimi is proud of the role he plays in facilitating suicide bombings, along with his standing among the local insurgency groups. "Many people in the insurgency know me," he noted, "even if they have never met me."

and place for the bombings, suicide bombers usually credit this choice to Allah as well. "We don't get to choose the mission," one said. "That is up to Allah." Frequently, suicide bombers learn when their mission will take place just minutes before they are sent out. While waiting to be called, suicide bombers try to tie up loose ends in their own lives. They pay off any debts they may owe, as well as resolve any important family matters that must be seen to. They ready themselves for the day they will meet Allah in Paradise. As one suicide-bomber-in-training summed up the essence of his existence, "The only person who matters is Allah—and the only question he will ask me is 'How many infidels [nonbelievers] did you kill?'"

An Iraqi flag is displayed at the entrance to the home a fourteen-year-old suicide bomber in order to welcome Rakad Salem, an ambassador from Saddam Hussein. Salem, who was arrested by the Israelis in October 2002, allegedly distributed nearly $25 million of Hussein's money to Palestinian families of "martyrs."

# Chapter 5
# THE FAMILIES
# OF SUICIDE BOMBERS

"If I had twenty children, I'd send them all off to Israel to blow themselves up and kill some Israelis." Those are the words of a Palestinian bricklayer whose son served as a suicide bomber in the spring of 2001. The man was all smiles following his child's assent to Paradise as a martyr. He told a reporter from Abu Dhabi TV that he did not regret losing his son because the boy took twenty-one Israelis to the grave with him.

The father's smiles, along with those of the other family members, continued during the buffet reception following the young martyr's death, at which tea, lemonade, and sweet honey cakes were served. Yet within weeks, the man's steely composure began to crumple. He soon found it hard to keep up his formerly cheerful demeanor.

Clearly, this loving father had begun to seriously question why he had to lose his son. When later interviewed by a reporter, the man took out a photo album filled with pictures of his son. Though he tried hard to hold back the tears, it was impossible for him to do so any longer. Trying desperately to make sense out of his son's death, the grief-stricken father cried, "I have to be proud of him." It was as if he did not feel that he had any other choice. According to Islam, martyrs are not to be mourned, but that did not seem to lessen the pain he felt.

Similar feelings among parents whose children have become suicide bombers are not uncommon. Nevertheless, extremist organizations do all they can to keep these reactions out of the press. They make it difficult for the suicide bomber's relatives not to conform to the image of a family filled with pride over their heroic son or daughter who is now in Paradise.

Over time, extremist organizations have developed techniques to try to soften the parents' grief over what has happened. Usually the family is showered with praise, gifts, and attention. In some instances, a family will be offered free education for their remaining children as well as free medical care. Often the parents receive large cash donations from Palestinian organizations, various Arabic leaders, and sympathizers throughout the region. The mother of one suicide bomber reported that following her son's death, she received $10,000 from former Iraqi president Saddam Hussein, $3,000 from the United Arab Emirates, and a few thousand more from Saudi Arabia and other Gulf states. Later, the amount given to each Palestinian suicide bomber's family by Saddam Hussein was raised to $25,000. Prior to his overthrow in Iraq, Hussein had given about $25 million to the families of Palestinian suicide bombers.

These families are encouraged not to think of the bombing as their child's death but rather as his ascent to Paradise and his wedding to the "black-eyed" virgins. To underscore that, instead of death notices, they place wedding announcements in the newspapers. One such notice in *Al-Istiqlal,* the Palestinian Authority paper, read, "With great pride, the Palestinian Islamic Jihad marries the member of its military wing . . . the martyr and hero Yasser Al-Adhami, to the 'black-eyed' [virgins]." The Hamas newspaper, *Al-Risala,* published the will of one of its suicide bombers. It encouraged the young man's mother to "call out in joy" and "distribute sweets" because of the wonderful wedding that awaits her son in Paradise.

Under pressure, many families may express pride in their child's martyrdom, but this is hardly what they feel. Leyla Atschan, a psychologist from Ramallah, has counseled the mothers of some suicide bombers and is familiar with the sadness that frequently lurks beneath the surface.

> "They always talk about how proud they are, yes, truly proud of their son's actions—but it almost physically pains me to hear how violently they have to keep their voices steady while they're talking, how they have to stop themselves from falling apart. . . . Wherever you visit the families of the 'human bombs' in Gaza, Nablus, Kamallah or Hebron, you always find the same veneer of pride, the same platitudes. The more distant the friends and relatives are, the more proud they are. But beneath the bluster, there's a kind of silence; the parents either say nothing, or say, 'What he did just has to have been right!'"

In other instances, the hurt and rage experienced by the parents of suicide bombers has been far less subtle. Even though many extremist groups claim that suicide bombers must inform their parents of their participation in jihad, apparently some of these young people fail to ask their parents' permission before blowing themselves up.

As the mother of a young suicide bomber who blew himself up in a Sbarro pizzeria in Israel in August 2001 said, "You think I would have let him go if I had known? I would have closed the house with a hundred locks before I would have let him go. What is Palestine going to give me? He's gone. . . . Nobody wants to lose a son in this world. Palestine is eating its children."

## YOU CAN CHOOSE YOUR FRIENDS BUT NOT YOUR RELATIVES

Fifteen-year-old Shireen Rabiya is a Palestinian teen from a fairly well-off family near Bethlehem. Her father owns both a convenience store and a chicken farm. Her mother described Shireen's life: "She is the youngest and was sheltered. She never suffered or wanted for anything." Yet the adolescent girl was not as happy as she would have liked to be, because some of the students at her school teased her about being taller and thinner than the other girls.

One day, Shireen happened to meet her uncle on the street, and as they spoke, Shireen mentioned that she was sometimes teased. Her uncle agreed that it must be hard for her, but after they parted that day, Shireen thought no more about it. She was surprised when, the following week, her uncle showed up at her school. The principal called her out of class, and he and her uncle suggested that Shireen become a suicide bomber. Shireen was told that after being fitted for an explosive belt, she would be taken to Jerusalem to blow herself up. They said that the bombing would be over quickly, and then she would wake up in Paradise. Her uncle convinced Shireen that in Paradise she would be popular in school and would always get good grades.

On the other hand, the militants who sent her son to die in the Israeli pizza parlor were quite pleased with the deed. They hoped his mission would send a chilling message to the people of Israel. The militants wanted the Israelis to know that they could no longer feel safe anywhere. As Munir al Makdah, a jihadist who has run training camps for would-be martyrs, put it, "They [the Israelis] shall be a target for all our freedom fighters. . . . They are not allowed to walk in the streets in peace. They are not allowed to eat pizza."

Shireen found the idea exciting and agreed to do it. "I never thought about doing it for the Palestinian state," Shireen recalled. "He [her uncle] never mentioned anything like that. I only thought about Paradise and that . . . everyone would like me."

Her uncle was later arrested by the Israelis for his involvement with terrorist organizations. When interviewed from prison and asked about Shireen, he said, "Her life on earth was worthless, and there was no doubt in my mind that she would have a more rewarding existence in the after-life."

Shireen never completed her bombing mission, as Israeli forces learned of it beforehand. When asked why she ever agreed to become a suicide bomber, Shireen replied, "I don't know. It sounded like fun. It sounded exciting and so many others had done it or tried that I thought, why not me?" Later on, Shireen added that she had always wanted to marry and be a mother. She said, "I never wanted to die. Things just happened so quickly that I never realized what I was doing when I agreed to the plan that my uncle suggested."

Shireen's mother deeply resented what her brother-in-law, Shireen's uncle, tried to do. "He had no right to involve my daughter," she firmly stated. "He has children of his own."

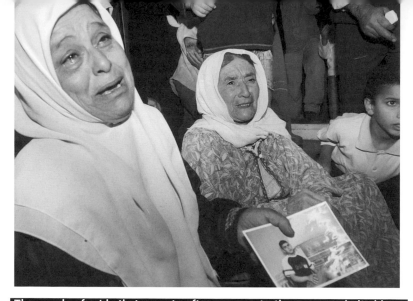

The words of pride that parents often express to the press are belied by the grief of losing their sons and daughters. Here, a stricken family holds a picture of twenty-year-old suicide bomber Hassan Abu Zeid, who blew himself up at a falafel stand in Hadera, Israel, in October 2005, killing himself and five Israelis.

As the number of suicide bombings increased in both Iraq and Israel, many Muslim parents became exceedingly concerned. They wanted to know what they could do to prevent their children from getting caught up in what they regarded as a growing and very disturbing trend. Many parents have asked mental health experts to help them identify early-warning signs in their children that might make them open to taking such extreme measures.

"This has been happening more and more often in the last few months as the Palestinian resistance has deepened," noted Dr. Mahmud Sehwail, a psychologist and director of a mental health center in Ramallah in a June, 2002, interview. "The parents say they have detected a significant change in the behavior of their children, and they desperately want to know if their children are candidates to become human bombs."

In one instance, a seventeen-year-old Palestinian girl who

# WITHOUT THEIR CONSENT

While suicide bombers supposedly volunteer for their missions and ideally should have their parents' blessings, this is not always the case. It certainly was not true for twelve-year-old Abdullah Quran, who on March 16, 2004, was tricked into carrying a sizable bomb in his backpack to the Israeli checkpoint near Nablus. The only reason Abdullah Quran is still alive is because the bomb malfunctioned and did not detonate. As it turned out, the young boy did not even know that he was carrying a bomb. He thought that he was just taking some car parts to a woman on the other side of the checkpoint.

A similar incident occurred about a week later. This sixteen-year-old boy (with a mental age of twelve) was stopped at an Israeli checkpoint wearing an eighteen-pound suicide bomber's vest. Husam Abdo, the young Palestinian, tearfully told Israeli soldiers that he did not want to die or be blown up. His parents, who did not know that militants had strapped the bomb to their son, were furious. Two hundred to three hundred innocent Palestinians waiting at the checkpoint could have been killed or badly hurt as well.

Palestinian youth Hussam Abdo is caught on camera as he approaches a crowded checkpoint wearing a suicide bomb vest. Soldiers sent a robot carrying scissors to the boy so he could cut off the vest.

wanted to become a suicide bomber ran away from home to do so. If her father had not taken some quick action, she might have been accepted by an extremist organization and begun the standard indoctrination and training to complete this deadly task. "The father called the Palestinian security officials and the Israeli security officials," Dr. Sehwail remarked in describing what happened, "and just a few days ago, the girl was found safe and sound and her suicide was averted."

Fearful that this could happen again, the girl's parents took steps to see that it did not. They made sure that she got the psychological counseling she needed to better handle her anger and depression. It seems that her cousin had recently been killed by Israeli soldiers, and the girl had been more affected by this than her parents first realized.

However, on the whole, Dr. Sehwail feels that this is a new trend that seems to be getting stronger. He sees it as a battle between militants and parents over the lives of Palestinian youths. Um Iyad, the mother of a suicide bomber, wishes that she had known her son's intentions so that she could have fought the militants for his life.

It is not that these parents do not share their children's feelings of frustration and powerlessness. They just do not share the belief that blowing yourself up is the answer. In the words of Dr. Eyad Sarraj, founder and director of the Gaza Community Mental Health Programme, "We're all powerless here, but some can bear it while others can't."

Some parents of suicide bombers also find the idea of killing Israeli civilians particularly offensive. Though they feel wronged, they do not think that killing innocent Israeli children will ever make up for their loss. In evaluating her son's actions as a suicide bomber, Um Iyad sighs and says, "I have to say that it was not a good thing that he did. There were many innocents there [at the establishment he bombed]. So many children. We don't support it when the Israelis kill our people, so we can't support it when their innocent people are killed. We just can't condone that kind of martyrdom."

On April 11, 1945, the U.S. battleship *Missouri* opened fire on a low-flying Japanese suicide plane. The plane crashed just below her main deck level, and the battleship suffered only superficial damage.

# Chapter 6
## KAMIKAZE—
## SPECIAL ATTACK FORCES

While many Muslim parents of suicide bombers grieve over the loss of their children, they are not the first to do so. At different times throughout history, young people in various societies have knowingly gone to their death for God and country. The most notable example in modern history occurred during World War II (1939–1945), when thousands of young Japanese men volunteered to serve as kamikaze pilots— aviators in special military units designed to conduct suicide missions. The kamikaze units were formed toward the end of World War II to stop the United States from making further significant gains against Japan. It was a desperate time for the Japanese. Their wartime losses had been extremely high.

The name *kamikaze* comes from a Japanese legend. According to the legend, twice in the late 1200s the Mongolian conqueror Kublai Khan sent large fleets to invade Japan. Both times the fleets were destroyed by typhoons believed to have been sent by the sun goddess and storm god. These divine interventions became known as the kamikaze or the "divine wind." In World War II, the name was given to the young pilots who were supposed to destroy the U.S. invasion force as the typhoons had destroyed Kublai Khan's fleets centuries earlier.

Kamikaze pilots were trained to turn their aircraft into powerful flying bombs as they crashed into the enemy target with the greatest possible speed and force. No kamikaze pilots were expected to survive—when they went out on a mission, they did not come back. The first kamikaze attack took place in the fall of 1944, and by the time the attacks were over in April 1945, thousands of young Japanese pilots had lost their lives. They managed to sink 120 U.S. ships and damaged many more. Approximately 3,050 Allied servicemen were killed as a result of the kamikaze attacks, and another 6,025 were wounded.

How could a nation expect its young men to make the ultimate sacrifice and proudly go to their deaths? This brings up some interesting parallels with suicide bombers in the Middle East. In both the Middle East and Japan, the suicide bombers felt that their land, religion, or way of life was threatened by an outside power. In the case of the Palestinian suicide bombers, it is the Israeli occupation; in Iraq, it is the continued presence of American troops long after Saddam Hussein was removed from power.

The Japanese also felt threatened by the power of the American military during World War II. Fighting the Americans had taken a heavy toll on Japanese forces. Before long, Japan was facing an increasing number of American attacks with a shortage of both planes and ships. To worsen the situation, at the time, Japan also had a shortage of well-trained pilots. Just as suicide bombers in the Middle East tend to be young, many of the Japanese boys who trained to be kamikaze pilots during World War II were between fourteen and seventeen years old. Although, technically, pilots under seventeen were not to be sent into combat, due to the shortage, many as young as fourteen went. These hastily trained youths were considerably less skilled than the U.S. pilots they were up against.

Vice-Admiral Takajiro Ohnishi is generally credited with forming the special attack force known as the kamikaze. These young pilots became the hope of the Japanese military. Everyone expected them to turn things around for Japan during these desperate times. Ohnishi has been quoted as saying,

> There are only two types of airmen in the world, the winners and the losers. And even though Japan is suffering from a serious shortage of trained pilots, there is a remedy for this. If a pilot, facing a ship or plane, exhausts all his resources, then he still has one left, the plane as part of himself, a superb weapon. And what greater glory can there be than to give your life for Emperor and country?

The Japanese vice-admiral's proposal is not unlike much of the reasoning given for using suicide bombers in the Middle East. There, suicide bombers claim that they are ready to give their lives to defend Islam. The Japanese kamikaze pilots were supposedly willing to die for their emperor. While the emperor of Japan was not considered a living god, he was believed to be a descendant of the sun goddess and therefore divine.

Many young Japanese men had wanted to be pilots at the start of the war. They had grown up hearing tales of the Samurai—the warrior class in Japan famous for being valiant and fearless fighters. These tales were part of their cultural heritage, and young Japanese boys dreamed of being as brave and honorable in war as the Samurai of the past were.

Toward the end of World War II, the Japanese fighters needed all the courage they could muster. The American military was closing in, and without sufficient planes and trained pilots to fly them, the situation looked bleak. For months, the officers in the Japanese high military command had continued discussing the idea of developing a kamikaze attack force. But not all the chief military officers were in agreement on the idea.

Some were against having a kamikaze force due to the tremendous loss of life these operations would entail. Others, in favor of such a force, argued that in fighting the Americans, the chances of a pilot returning alive were extremely slim anyway. Not only were the American pilots more knowledgeable and better trained, but U.S. weaponry and planes were far superior as well. The Japanese military high command reasoned that if their pilots were bound to die, they might as well be put to the best use possible. Vice-Admiral Ohnishi perhaps best summed up the situation when he said, "In my opinion, there is only one way of assuring that our meager strength will be effective to a maximum degree. That is to organize suicide attack units of Zero fighters, armed with 250-kilogram bombs, each plane to crash-dive into the enemy carrier. . . ."

The idea was to inflict the greatest possible damage on the enemy while using the fewest resources to do so. However, before they could proceed further, the Japanese high command had to be sure that their pilots would go along with the idea. Therefore, the question was put to the 201st Air Group—a unit of aviators that had suffered some tremendous losses. At that point, these young pilots were both exhausted and discouraged. American anti-aircraft artillery and fighter planes had consistently downed the group's planes. Many of the pilots in the 201st Air Group did not expect to return home from the war alive, and they wanted to be remembered as fighters who bravely fought for their country. When asked if they were willing to die to save the Japanese Empire, every man in the 201st volunteered for kamikaze duty.

Once these young pilots were dead, other units volunteered to take their place. As Hamas and other organizations in the

This photo shows former kamikaze pilot Toshio Yoshitake (far right) and his fellow pilots posing before taking off from Tokyo on a mission. None of the seventeen other pilots and flight instructors who flew with Yoshitake on that day survived. Yoshitake himself is alive only because a U.S. warplane shot him out of the air, and he crash-landed and was rescued by Japanese soldiers.

Middle East found, there was no shortage of young people who hoped to become suicide bombers. The young Japanese pilots had been brought up to believe that courage, loyalty, discipline, and self-sacrifice were what mattered. To refuse to die for their country would bring such overwhelming disgrace to themselves and their families that some might feel their lives were no longer worth living. Therefore, these young men avoided this catastrophic consequence and bravely volunteered with the others they had trained with.

Here again, there are similarities to the present-day suicide bombings taking place in the Middle East. During a suicide bomber's indoctrination in the Middle East, the young person continually hears what an important contribution his or her suicide bombing is to the cause. The kamikazes in Japan had a similar experience. These young aviators lived in military barracks with other flyers who had strong warrior values. They formed a solid peer group that would not readily accept a change of heart from one of the volunteers.

In the Middle East as well as in Japan, there was also the promise of a wonderful afterlife awaiting those who engaged in suicide bombings. The Muslim bombers believe that they are going to Paradise. The kamikaze pilots believed that following their death, they would become a small god or spirit called an *Eirei*. Their final resting place was to be the Yasukuni Jima—a Shinto temple in Tokyo reserved for heroes.

Still another similarity between suicide bombers in the Middle East and the Japanese kamikaze pilots of World War II is that both were also given very specific instructions on how to behave during the last moments of their life. The Middle Eastern bombers are told to cry out "Allah Akhbar or "God is great" before detonating themselves. Kamikaze pilots received very precise directions on how to appear just before crashing

## FUELING A KAMIKAZE MISSION

There were different theories about how to best fuel a kamikaze plane. At the start of the war effort, most pilots liked to make sure that their fuel tanks were filled to the brim prior to takeoff. They hoped to inflict the maximum amount of damage to the enemy target that way. At the moment of impact, the additional burning fuel would intensify the explosion.

There was a secondary benefit to flying with a full fuel tank as well. The pilot had enough fuel to get back if for some reason the mission needed to be called off at the last minute. This sometimes occurred if the target was out of range or if the pilot was experiencing some mechanical difficulties with his aircraft. Such mishaps did not reflect poorly on the pilot, who was usually sent out again a few days later on a hopefully more successful mission.

However, as the war progressed and fuel shortages became a problem, the kamikaze pilots were forced to change their tactics. At times, these pilots were sent out with barely enough fuel to reach their intended targets. This robbed the pilot of any flexibility in altering the course of a mission. It was clear that these pilots were not going to return—whether they reached their targets or not.

their planes. Incredibly, they were told to always smile and look enthusiastic.

On the surface, it might seem like every young Japanese pilot was unconditionally brave and ready to die for his emperor and country. Yet a closer examination of the situation reveals a more complex picture. At least some of these men had second thoughts about becoming suicide bombers that they felt unable to voice or act on. Their mixed feelings about these deadly missions became apparent in some of the letters, writings, and poems kamikaze pilots left for their relatives. At times, these suggest what might have been really going on in the minds of these young pilots just before their date with death.

The following note was written by a kamikaze pilot who knew that this would be the last letter his parents and sisters would ever receive from him. In it, he lets them know how much he'll miss their tenderness and affection:

> My dear parents, I shall depart this life at 0700 hours on the twenty-ninth of June, 1945. My whole being is permeated by your tremendous affection, down to the last hair. And it is this which is hard to accept: the thought that with my carnal disappearance [death], this tenderness will also disappear. But patriotic duty demands it. I sincerely beg your pardon for not carrying out my filial [family] duties to the very end. Please remember me to all those who have shown me friendship and kindness.
>
> Dear sisters, farewell! Our parents no longer have a son. It must therefore be your task to give them every loving care during their lifetime. Always be kind and gracious, worthy of Japanese womanhood.

Another young pilot who was upset over having to serve as a suicide bomber had the courage to admit in his writings that he was afraid of dying. Reading his words, we get the feeling that he would have liked to find a way out of going on the mission, but seeing none, he resigned himself to his fate. He wrote:

> Fear plagues me. I ask myself: "Will I suffer at the moment of the explosion?" I answer at once: "Ugh! It's not worth thinking about. The pain will only last a flash, perhaps a tenth of a second. . . ." The sea below is rough and grey [he

was flying that day]. The high white waves are like fabulous beasts showing their teeth. But at least, this is the manifestation of nature, of life, and when I consider that soon I shall have no contact with these things, I find the angry swell and foam pleasing to the eye. I feel a profound attachment to life surging up anew in me, lacerating my heart, as death approaches closer and closer. I am fully conscious of it. I long to cry out: "Why me? Why must I die, when my fellow students are allowed to live, and will be able to resume their studies?" There is no answer, no solution. Man is too weak to accept an accomplished fact without regret.

**In 1945 a *Time-Life* photographer captured an image of a kamikaze pilot writing his last letter home before embarking on his suicide mission.**

But I am no longer a student, I am a suicide-pilot. I am about to crash-dive on the enemy without hope of return. What is the good of struggling with myself? I say resignedly: "Farewell, nature! Farewell, world!"

In some cases, having a son selected as a suicide bomber meant financial hardship for a family as well as the emotional pain that losing a child can bring. At first, the commanding officers tried not to select pilots who were their family's "only son" for suicide bombing missions. However, as the number of trained pilots grew scarcer, these young men were used on kamikaze missions as well. The concern and pain this sometimes entailed is evident in this firsthand account of a suicide bomber's last visit with his family. In this case, the young man decided not to tell his mother and sisters that he had been selected for a kamikaze mission as he felt it would be easier for them that way.

In the early afternoon, a happy surprise—my mother and two of my sisters came to visit me! . . . I thought my mother looked tired; no doubt feeding my family was a great worry to her. The country people were not very obliging [helpful] and I felt sorry for her with all my heart. Doubtless, the haunting fear of my death added to her burdens. I, her only son, was soon to die. She was condemned to live with her memories, whereas I, reduced to nothing would feel neither pain or joy, and would have no memories. In a sense, I was the luckier of the two.

My sisters questioned me anxiously: "Are you too among the suicide pilots?" I was disconcerted. It was better that my family should know nothing. I replied hastily that I was just another pilot. . . . I went to fetch my diary and my tortoise-shell cigarette case my eldest sister had given me. I gave them these objects, as if I were bequeathing them to them after my death, saying as I could: "Mother, here is my diary, it contains all my thoughts. If my C.O. [commanding officer] read it, he would punish me severely. . . ." [As the kamikaze were not allowed to reveal their true feelings regarding their missions.]

This would be our last meeting. . . . I accompanied them as far as the Kagohara Station. . . . In my secret being, I was bidding them farewell. . . . I had to struggle to keep back my tears. . . . I left the station and made my way back along the path I had just walked down with my mother. I looked for the trace of her footprints.

In the end, the kamikaze pilots were not the magical answer the Japanese military high command had hoped they would be. The kamikaze units failed to reverse the course of the war, and Japan was defeated by the United States. Nevertheless, between five thousand and seven thousand kamikaze flights were completed, resulting in the loss of thousands of young Japanese pilots. Just before Japan was forced to surrender, Vice-Admiral Takajiro Ohnishi killed himself. He left a note saying how sorry he was that the kamikaze pilots had died in vain. Ironically, only about one quarter of the kamikaze pilots ever managed to hit a ship before being shot down. Looking back on the era, many people view the kamikaze flights as a terrible waste of human life. It is not hard to find people who feel the same way about suicide bombers in the Middle East.

Suicide bombers attacked the United States on September, 11, 2001, destroying the World Trade Center and damaging the Pentagon.

# Chapter 7
# IT COULD NEVER HAPPEN HERE

Most Americans—even those born after World War II—had heard of kamikaze pilots. There were stories and books about them, and they were featured in dozens of World War II movies. Yet in the United States, people generally thought of them as part of a past era in wartime history. No one imagined that one day suicide bombers might use aircraft to target buildings in American cities. The idea was preposterous—who would dare launch such an attack against the world's greatest superpower? After all, didn't the United States have the most sophisticated military and weaponry on Earth? Would anyone be foolish enough to risk the retaliation that such an attack would invite? The plot was simply too farfetched for even the most outlandish Hollywood movie.

Yet on September 11, 2001, that's precisely what happened. Early that morning, the American Airlines passenger jet Flight 11 out of Boston should have been well on its way to Los Angeles, California, but that was not the case. Instead, the

Boeing 767 had been hijacked, and at 8:45 A.M. it slammed into the north tower of New York City's World Trade Center. The airplane tore a huge hole in the building, leaving it ablaze.

As people saw footage of the crash on television, they could not believe their eyes. But that was just the start of a horrific day. Only eighteen minutes later, at 9:03 A.M., a second hijacked jet, United Airlines Flight 175 from Boston, hit the World Trade Center's south tower and exploded on impact. Now both towers were in flames.

The passengers, crew, and hijackers from the two jets had been instantly killed, as had many of those working in the towers. As others frantically tried to escape from the burning buildings, it seemed to some like the end of the world. There was nothing in their backgrounds to prepare them for this—Americans had always thought of their homeland as immune from attack. Just blocks from the World Trade Center, Ed Stawarz, the assistant director of building maintenance at the Federal Reserve Bank of New York, was on the roof with some coworkers when he saw the first jet heading straight for the north tower. He described what it was like this way:

> The jet was so close I could see the windows with people sitting in their seats. I could see the red and blue colors on the side and the big lettering. Nobody knew what to think. "Oh my God, this thing has got to go into the river," I said. Then all of a sudden the roar of the engines got louder. This guy was intentionally gunning for the World Trade Center. It went right into the side of the building. It was like the tower just consumed the jet. It went HHSSHHLLIITT! Just sucked it inside. It was some sight, I will tell you. I saw the tail end going and going and then it

was all gone. . . . I was just stuck there for a moment in horror and shock. You can't believe what you just saw.

Not knowing what might be next, authorities tried to stop any further incidents. At 9:17 A.M., the Federal Aviation Administration shut down all New York airports, and shortly thereafter the Port Authority of New York and New Jersey ordered New York's bridges and tunnels closed. Then at 9:40 A.M., the Federal Aviation Administration suspended flight operations at airports throughout the United States. Nationwide air traffic was stopped for the first time in the country's history.

Unfortunately, even these measures came too late. Other hijacked airplanes piloted by suicide bombers were already in the air. At 9:43 A.M., American Airlines Flight 77 crashed into the Pentagon, sending up a huge cloud of smoke that permeated the air. Evacuation of the building began immediately, but not everyone was saved. By 10:00 A.M., a fourth hijacked plane, United Airlines Flight 93, had been diverted from its route to San Francisco and was headed for the nation's capital. However, passengers on Flight 93 fought the hijackers, and the plane crashed into a field in Somerset County, Pennsylvania, southeast of Pittsburgh. In a cell phone call to his wife just before the passengers tackled the hijackers, a man on board the plane said that he knew that they were all going to die, but that they had to do something. They did, and by having the plane crash in a field, it is likely that many lives were spared. As President George W. Bush would later characterize their bravery, "They [the passengers on Flight 93] told their loved ones they loved them, they said a prayer, one guy said 'let's roll' and they drove an airplane in the ground to serve something greater than themselves in life."

Meanwhile, the numbers of dead were already mounting in New York and Washington, DC. Before 10:30 A.M. both the north and south towers of the World Trade Center collapsed, releasing a tremendous cloud of debris and smoke that blanketed the area. At a press conference later that afternoon, when New York City Mayor Rudolph Giuliani was asked about the number of people killed, he said, "I don't think we want to speculate about that—(it is) more than any of us can bear."

Still not knowing whether there was more to come, five warships and two aircraft carriers were sent out from the U.S. Naval Station in Norfolk, Virginia, to protect the east coast of the United States. The guided missile destroyers were capable of shooting down planes. In addition, the Immigration and Naturalization Service placed the U.S. borders on the highest state of alert. Addressing the American public from Barksdale Air Force Base in Louisiana just after 1:00 P.M., President George W. Bush told the nation, "Make no mistake, the United States will hunt down and punish those responsible for these cowardly acts."

In the months ahead, Americans learned that this was easier said than done. The suicide bombers responsible for what became known as 9/11 proved to be nineteen young men who carried out the wishes of the highly effective yet elusive international terrorist leader Osama bin Laden. Bin Laden, an Islamic extremist, believes that through the years, U.S. support has allowed secular governments to survive in Muslim nations. With the ultimate goal of driving all Westerners out of Muslim lands, he would like to see these governments replaced by Islamic fundamentalist regimes that would interpret the Koran in its strictest sense. Bin Laden believes that Western corruption could taint the purity of Muslim society and feels that the United States is the main enemy of the Muslim faith.

Osama bin Laden is seen on television October 7, 2001, praising Allah for the September 11 attacks on America and swearing that America will never be able to feel secure until its armies leave Muslim lands.

On numerous occasions since 1998, he has declared war on the United States.

Osama bin Laden's organization, al-Qaeda, is known to be active throughout the Middle East, as well as in at least fifteen other nations, including Spain, England, the Netherlands, Russia, and the Philippines. Some sources suggest that bin Laden's reach is even more global, as many terrorist subgroups have merged into a network with larger groups that are often either inspired by or loosely connected to al-Qaeda. According to the British journal *Jane's Intelligence Review,* al-Qaeda has access to thousands of members spread across more than fifty countries. It serves as an inspiration and guide for numerous extremist organizations that hope to purge Muslim states of all Western influence. David Long, a terrorism specialist, described al-Qaeda as follows: "This is not an organization of terrorists in the traditional sense. It is more like a gathering place for diverse subgroups to obtain financing, support, and military training. It's a chameleon, an amoeba, that constantly changes form and color but has only one leader: Osama bin Laden."

A psychological profile of the nineteen suicide bombers responsible for 9/11 showed that these men had more in common with one another than just being young and Muslim. They were also intelligent, well educated, and largely from middle-class homes. Yet besides these things, the hijackers may have shared some other characteristics that allowed them to become mass-murderers that sunny September morning. While these traits may have been especially evident in Mohamed Atta, the thirty-three-year-old Egyptian-born ringleader, they existed in the other suicide bombers as well.

All the 9/11 suicide bombers had developed an extreme religious and political belief system that they rigidly held to. An intense preoccupation with his religion was among the first things people noticed about Atta, the suicide bomber believed to have led the attack on the World Trade Center by piloting American Airlines Flight 11 into the north tower. At times, Atta's hard religious stance got in the way of his relationships with others. This was obvious during the time he spent working and studying in Hamburg, Germany, while living with a German host family. The situation is described in the book *Inside 9-11: What Really Happened:*

> Five times a day he [Atta] took over the bathroom to wash himself, and afterward he ran to his room with arms upstretched in prayer—lest  he come into contact with the

unclean family dog. He closed his eyes when his hostess wore her nightgown and he pretended her [female] friends did not exist. . . . During the month of Ramadan, Atta would not eat anything before sundown. He started cooking at night. "That's when we asked him to leave," his hosts say.

A number of the young men involved in the 9/11 suicide bombings were part of a terrorist cell in Germany with Atta. They prayed together regularly at local mosques in Hamburg. While there, the group was also known to sit apart from others whom they believed did not share their radical views.

Another characteristic shared by the 9/11 suicide bombers was a rigid view of Westerners and Jews as the enemy. Mohamed Atta had grown up in Cairo, Egypt, where even as a young boy, he disliked Americans. His father had nothing but contempt for the United States, which he felt was an aggressive and corrupt nation, intent on taking over much of the world. "Sooner or later they'll [the Americans] occupy Egypt," he would warn his young son Mohamed.

Atta, who later studied urban planning, hated how the West had influenced architecture in his homeland. He intensely disliked the high-rises, modern hotel chains, and fast-food outlets that dotted the Egyptian landscape. Atta regretted the "decline of the old residential buildings" in Cairo and did not want his country to become "Mc-Egypt."

Atta, along with the other 9/11 suicide bombers, detested Jews as well as Americans. Those who were part of the terrorist cell in Germany made no secret of their feelings. At times, while at Hamburg mosques, they would shout out, "Let the Jews burn. We'll dance on their graves."

Lastly, the 9/11 suicide bombers all believed that a holy war was being waged against the West and that their suicide bombings were a necessary military tactic. This might have been the main unifying thread among the 9/11 suicide bombers. Some had attended al-Qaeda training camps, where they were schooled in various terrorist tactics and their commitment to the holy war was solidified. Abdulaziz al-Omari was on American Airlines Flight 11 and helped Mohamed Atta crash the plane into the World Trade Center. As early as the spring of 2001, al-Omari made his farewell video, in which he thanked Osama bin Laden for training him and acknowledged that the end was near.

Ziad Jarrah was one of the hijackers on board the plane that

On September 11, 2001, a security camera at Portland International Airport caught 9/11 hijackers Mohammed Atta (right) and Abdulaziz al-Omari as they passed through airport security to catch a commuter flight to Boston.

Waleed M. Alsheri

Mohammed Atta

Wail M. Alshehri

Abdulaziz Alomari

Satam M.A. al-Suqami

Undated photos of the suspected hijackers of American Airlines Flight 11 that crashed into the World Trade Center. They are (top row, left to right) Waleed M. Alsheri, Mohammed Atta, and Wail M. Alsheri, (bottom row, left to right) Abdulaziz al-Omari and Satam M. A. al-Suqami.

crashed into the Pennsylvania field on 9/11. Like the other suicide bombers, he was committed to Osama bin Laden and to waging a holy war. Jarrah once told his great-uncle that his life's purpose was to be a martyr. This comment reflected the real strength of Jarrah's commitment because in one very special way he was not like the other hijackers. Twenty-six-year-old Ziad Jarrah was in love. His girlfriend was a beautiful young Turkish woman who was studying to be a doctor.

# THE SHOE BOMBER

Following the September 11 terrorist attacks, it took months before many Americans truly felt comfortable flying again. Yet by December, more people began to take to the air for some holiday travel. They were not alone in doing so, however. On December 22, 2001, Richard Reid, a tall British man who had recently become a Muslim, boarded American Airlines Flight 63 from Paris to Miami.

Reid, a would-be suicide bomber, had explosives tightly packed into his athletic shoes. While the plane was in flight, a passenger saw him trying to light a wire extending from the inner tongue of his shoe. The explosion was stopped due to some quick thinking from the passengers and crew, who realized what Reid was up to in time. Though he put up a fight, he was finally subdued and restrained with seat belt extensions. Two French physicians on board injected Reid with sedatives to keep him quiet until the aircraft landed.

It was later revealed that Reid was not acting alone. Authorities learned that he was an al-Qaeda-trained terrorist. In an e-mail to his mother, Reid described himself as a fighter against "oppressive" U.S. forces in Muslim nations. Files from a computer seized from al-Qaeda backed up his claim. These indicated that Reid might have

Though he kept this relationship secret from his strict Muslim parents, friends of Jarrah claim that he was very taken with this woman and that the couple had discussed marriage. Nevertheless, Jarrah's identification with the group and his indoctrination won out, and he became a suicide bomber.

Jarrah's choice was not as unusual as it may seem. In the months prior to 9/11, all the suicide bombers saw themselves as soldiers in a holy war to defend their faith. As seen through their behavior, in some ways, joining an extremist Islamic been sent out on special trips to identify possible targets to attack. Reid's own travel schedule showed that in the months prior to the attempted shoe bombing, he had traveled to Israel, Egypt, Turkey, and Pakistan. As these are costly trips and Reid had no known source of income, authorities believe that an al-Qaeda-related terrorist group financed his travels.

Richard Reid was later tried in a U.S. court and sentenced to life in prison.

**Born in 1973, Richard Reid was the son of an English mother and a Jamaican father. By the mid-1990s, Reid had fallen into a life of petty crime and had already been jailed for several muggings.**

group is like joining a cult. The young people involved in the 9/11 attacks gave up thinking for themselves. They forfeited their individuality for what they believed was the higher purpose of the group's goals. Suicide bombers come to believe that their value as human beings is directly tied to how effectively they carry out their mission.

On October 12, 2002, in the town of Kura on the Indonesian island of Bali, a suicide bomber exploded a bomb in a popular tourtist bar. As survivors poured out of the bar, a car bomb detonated just outside. A third bomb went off in front of the American Embassy. The deadliest act in Indonesian history, the bombs killed 202 people and injured 209.

## Chapter 8
# GONE GLOBAL—SUICIDE BOMBERS THROUGHOUT THE WORLD

If you think that suicide bombers are largely just a problem in Israel and Iraq, think again. The phenomenon of turning human beings into bombs has gone global in recent years, making suicide bombings a problem in many parts of the world. Besides occurring in Israel and Iraq, there have been reports of suicide bombings in Bali, Egypt, Argentina, Lebanon, Sri Lanka, Turkey, the Philippines, and other areas.

The use of suicide bombers has recently become popular in the Republic of Chechnya, a Muslim region that's been actively engaged in an ongoing struggle for independence from Russia. For years Russia has fought against Chechnya's secession, but the Chechnyan struggle continues.

By the year 2000, Chechen rebels had suicide bombers using car bombs to blow up carefully selected military targets. These bombers were usually young males. Then in 2003, the rebels started using suicide bombers in strikes against civilian targets. At this point, women were also allowed to serve as suicide bombers. Rebel forces even had special training camps set up for females, which were run by Arab instructors who had come to Chechnya. As Mia Bloom described in her book, *Dying to Kill: The Allure of Suicide Terror:*

> Arab mercenaries are preparing female suicide bombers for terror acts in Chechnya. . . . According to [Russian intelligence sources] no less than 30 women, most of them wives or relatives of Chechen rebels and even field commanders, are currently being prepared in training camps located, primarily, in the mountainous regions of Chechnya. They are being prepared by Arab instructors. . . . Female terrorists, who have completed the course, have already conducted a number of attacks. . . . "

In the summer of 2004, two women carrying bombs boarded separate planes at a Russian airport near Moscow. Once the planes were in flight, the women detonated the explosives, bringing both aircrafts down. A week later, a woman believed to be the younger sister of one of the airplane bombers blew herself up in front of a subway, killing 10 and injuring 51.

Women were also involved in the rebel siege of a Russian school in Beslan, where over three hundred people were killed by the time the 3-day seige ended with a final gun battle between the hostage takers and Russian security forces. Though some of the rebels on this mission wore vests containing explosives, others draped bombs over the building's ceiling beams. After telling the terrified hostages what might happen, the rebels concluded by saying, " . . . and then [we will] blow ourselves up. We have nothing to lose. We came here to die."

Though the Chechens are predominantly Muslims and are believed to have been assisted by groups connected to

Hostages sit on the floor surrounding a terrorist. He is working on what appears to be an explosive device in this image taken during the September 2004 Beslan school siege.

al-Qaeda, in some ways they are quite different from the extremist Muslim groups of the Middle East. The Chechens have not embraced the whole concept of religious martyrdom as it relates to suicide bombers. There are no posters or feasts celebrating martyrs there. Those who become suicide bombers do so as part of the fight to win their country's independence, not because they hope to go to Paradise.

The female suicide bombers, known as the Black Widows, sometimes say that they act out of a need for revenge. These women want to avenge the deaths of their husbands, brothers, and cousins at Russian hands. One female suicide bomber, who had lost both her husband and brother, said, "I have nothing to lose, I have nobody left. So I'll go all the way with this, even though I don't think it's the right thing to do."

Suicide bombings are not just occurring in Russia. In July 2005, the international community was shaken by the news that four suicide bombers had struck the transportation system in London, England. The attack occurred on July 7, 2005, during the early-morning rush hour. Four young male suicide bombers armed with backpacks containing bombs caused three explosions in London's underground subway system and one on a double-decker bus. The incident claimed the lives of fifty-two people and wounded more than seven hundred others.

Forty-nine-year-old London bus driver George Psaradakis described what it was like on the street that morning: "It was oddly silent, with a lot of distressed people crying into each other's arms. The top of the bus was lifted off, like the top of a tin can that's just been ripped open. There was smoke everywhere." Caught in the aftermath of the dust, smoke, fire, and twisted metal, victims of the blast struggled to understand why this had happened to them. Others, at home in Britain and the United States, saw the carnage on television and wondered why as well.

A group calling itself the Secret Organization Group of al-Qaeda of Jihad Organization in Europe claimed responsibility for the brutal act and issued the following statement: "Britain is burning with fear, terror, and panic in its northern, southern, eastern, and western quarters." After hearing this, the actual identity of the suicide bombers stunned authorities. While they had expected them to be from distant Arab lands, all four proved to be British citizens. They were not on any terrorist "watch lists" and did not have lengthy criminal records. In short, before July 7, 2005, they would not have been considered "bad people" by any standards.

CAMERA 14
07:21:54 07/07/05

A security camera outside of a London subway station captured the images of the four bombers entering the Luton station together at 7:21 A.M. on July 7, 2005.

Yet the claim of responsibility from an al-Qaeda related group and the fact that all the bombers happened to be young British Muslims did not go unnoticed by authorities. Over the years, tensions had often run high in Britain's Muslim community. At times, young males had rioted to protest the lack of employment and other opportunities available to the country's two million Muslims.

Moderate Muslim groups believe that these factors make their youths especially vulnerable to extremist propaganda. As Dr. Daud Abdullah of the Muslim Council of Britain put it, "We have social exclusion, we have a sense of not-belonging, a sense of alienation. We have alien ideas, frustration, and humiliation. When you add the international dimension to this, all these factors feed into the mindset of our youth, and it's demonstrating itself in this outrageous behavior."

It is likely that the four suicide bombers were dissatisfied Muslim youths who, while looking for some deeper meaning and a sense of belonging, had drifted toward the radical groups. They may have come in contact with extremists at the local community center near their homes, where militant views were often expressed. At least one of the suicide bombers is known to have played soccer there.

## DEALING WITH SUICIDE BOMBERS

Finding ways to handle suicide bombings is becoming increasingly necessary. The United States, as well as other nations, will need to take steps to minimize the impact of possible attacks. Israel, which has had to contend with increasingly frequent suicide bomber attacks since 2000, has adopted measures that are becoming standard procedure in an increasingly dangerous world. Some of these precautions are already being implemented in the United States. They are as follows:

• Learn as much as possible about the suicide bomber's operational network. Rather than focus on the bomber, concentrate on those who made the bomb, picked the target, and trained the bomber. Learn what these groups need to know to launch and perpetuate a suicide bombing campaign and be certain that information is shared with federal, state, and local authorities.

• Work to improve relations with the communities from which suicide bombers are most likely to come. In a nonthreatening way, antiterrorism units must encourage and cultivate cooperation with these community leaders. Attention and funding must be provided to lessen any genuine concerns in these areas.

In any case, before long, some of these young suicide bombers joined the ranks of the more than three thousand British Muslims who have gone to al-Qaeda training camps. One of the suicide bombers, Mohammed Sidique Khan, was known to have gone regularly to Pakistan as well as Afghanistan for military training. Another of the suicide bombers, eighteen-year-old Hasib Hussain, had not been a very good student at his school in London and often got into fights. However, after making a pilgrimage to Mecca and traveling to

- Sufficient funding must be made available to existing law enforcement agencies to identify suicide bombing plots before they are carried out. Special attention must be given to the places where suicide bombers are likely to be recruited, such as community centers, social clubs, schools, and religious institutions.

- Institute new training procedures to teach law enforcement officers how to identify a possible suicide bomber, confront a suspect, and secure the area around the attack site if an explosion should occur.

- Steps should be taken to ensure that ordinary materials are not turned into weapons in the event of an explosion. Windows on trains and buses should be shatterproof and seats strengthened so they are not easily dislodged. Protective barriers should be installed around vulnerable buildings and other structures.

- Merchants who sell materials that bombs can be made from— such as batteries, wires, or chemicals—should be trained to notify authorities if they see an unusually large purchase.

Pakistan, he became extremely devout. He grew a beard and began wearing traditional Muslim clothing. Shazad Tanweer, a third suicide bomber, had attended a radical school in Pakistan for a time as well.

Of course, the suicide bombers are only half the story. As usual, these four young men did not come up with the plot to bomb London's transportation system on their own. They were recruited and trained for the task. Supposedly, British recruits for these missions are not hard to find. A member of the extremist group Jaish-e-Muhammad (JEM) noted that Britain has long been a fruitful hunting ground for them. "It's an ideal situation," he said. "The young Muslims over there (in Britain) are not happy with the way Muslims are being treated and want to do something about it."

## SUICIDE BOMBERS IN SRI LANKA

Suicide bombing has gone on for decades in Sri Lanka, where the Sinhalese majority in the nation's south has discriminated against the Tamil people in the country's northeast. For years, the Tamils had been made to feel like second-class citizens in many ways. Sinhala, rather than English, was made the country's official language and the Tamils were unable to get jobs unless they learned Sinhala. Tamils were also frequently denied admission to institutions of higher learning, and few have been accepted into the army, which has frequently been reported as abusive to the Tamil minority.

Since the late 1970s, the Tamils have wanted to break away and form their own independent state. Militant Tamils began the Liberation Tigers of Tamil Eelam (LTTE) to stand up to the Sinhalese majority. In its fight for independence, LTTE has often resorted to using suicide bombers. Their male bombers are known as Black Tigers, and the female suicide bombers' wing is called Birds of Freedom.

While personal dissatisfaction may be at the root of why some young people are drawn to extremist groups, radical Muslim spokesmen prefer to give broader societal reasons for their actions. Sheik Omar Bakri Mohammad, an outspoken militant Islamic cleric, blamed the British government's actions for the London bombings. He noted, "Unless British foreign policy is changed and they withdraw forces [from all Muslim lands], I'm afraid there's going to be a lot of attacks. . . . " In describing the sentiments of young male Muslims in Britain today, he added, "They [the young Muslims] know that the [British] prime minister has his hands full of the blood of Muslims in Palestine and in Iraq and in Afghanistan."

The Sheik's prediction about future violence came true sooner than most expected. Two weeks to the day after the July

Suicide bombers in Sri Lanka tend to be young—most are between fourteen and sixteen years old. The LTTE also uses more females than adult males because women and young boys are less likely to be stopped and checked by authorities. It is also easier to hide a bulky suicide bomber's belt beneath the many layers of women's clothing. In addition, LTTE tries to save adult males for its combat forces. Suicide bombers in Sri Lanka train for about a year before being sent out to target important government officials as well as other people and places. So far, LTTE's suicide bombers have killed a president, a presidential candidate, the state minister of defense, the navy chief, and various other area commanders.

In interviews with suicide-bomber trainees, many indicated that they prefer death to living with oppression and hopelessness. According to one young trainee, "This is the most supreme sacrifice I can make. The only way we can get our Eelam [homeland] is through arms. This is the only way anybody will listen to us. Even if we die."

7 bombings, other bombers tried to stage a repeat performance of the attack. However, this time the bombs failed to explode, causing the young bombers to abandon their backpacks and flee from the scene. Though no one was hurt in this incident, Sir Ian Blair, chief of London's Metropolitan Police, bluntly stated the bombers' purpose when he said, "The intent must have been to kill."

The suicide bombings in London felt particularly threatening to Americans for a number of reasons. Sharing a common cultural viewpoint and a strong military alliance with Britain, Americans could not help but wonder when young people with bombs instead of books in their backpacks might make their way to our shores.

Guarding against suicide bombings is especially difficult in a free society where privacy and independence are cherished rights. Few Americans would want to see armed soldiers posted on street corners and in public buildings. Americans also do not want to have to carry identity papers with them and be subjected to random police searches. Accepting the risk of possible terrorist activity may be the price of living in a free and open society. Yet that risk must be acknowledged and dealt with. Following the news of the London bombings, some major American cities heightened security on their buses and trains. As early as March 2003, former Secretary of Homeland Security Tom Ridge warned that we have to "prepare for the inevitability" of suicide bombers on American soil. The London bombings made that inevitability seem just a little closer.

# SUICIDE BOMBINGS INCREASE IN AFGHANISTAN

The year 2006 saw a rise in the number of suicide bombings in Afghanistan. Often young bombers have been used in these attacks, like the one on an Afghan army vehicle on January 16 in downtown Kandahar.

Mohibar Rahman, a soldier, who was in the vehicle directly behind the one attacked, noted that the trouble had started when a teenage boy darted out in front of the convoy. "He lay down under the first vehicle," Rahman reported, "and blew himself up." Four soldiers and one civilian were killed in the bombing and another fourteen people were wounded.

In the past, suicide bombings had been relatively rare in Afghanistan, despite the ongoing strife there. However, recently things have begun to change. Both Afghan and foreign officials fear that Afghan terrorists may now be copying the terror tactics successfully used in Iraq.

Afghan terrorists are also employing more sophisticated marketing techniques to beef up the ongoing stream of fighters available to them. They produced an hour-long recruitment video called Lions of Islam. In it, masked guerilla fighters with AK47s and RPG launchers are shown at target practice—firing mortars and antiaircraft missiles. The terrorists' goal is to secretly distribute hundreds of thousands of these videos throughout Afghanistan, Pakistan, and many of the Gulf States. While some of the recruits will be assigned various duties within the terrorist organization's structure—others are likely to become suicide bombers.

As long as the death of a suicide bomber is regarded as something to celebrate, young people will continue to become the means by which their elders carry out political battles.

## Epilogue
# SUICIDE BOMBERS

In some ways, suicide bombers remain a puzzle. They defy being categorized. We have seen that they are not all poor, uneducated, and downtrodden. Many are highly intelligent, well educated, and from affluent homes. In addition, young people have sometimes volunteered to be suicide bombers for reasons that are not always apparent. At times, suicide bombers have actually been disillusioned or depressed teens who were drawn to a charismatic recruiter or who desperately needed a group's acceptance and approval. Some have been more interested in being seen as a hero after their death than in the cause they supposedly died for.

Apparently, extremist groups will send out young individuals to kill and be killed as easily as a soldier reloads his weapon. They have also convinced some youths that they would be happier dead than alive. As Suleiman Abu Gheith, al-Qaeda's chief spokesperson, said following 9/11, "Those youths that destroyed Americans with their planes, they did a good deed. There are thousands more young followers who look forward to death like Americans look forward to living." It may be hard to imagine young people who look forward to death the way American teens look forward to getting their driver's license or going to a prom. Yet given the often difficult circumstances of their lives, it is not inconceivable.

A neighbor of the suicide bombers who attacked London's transportation system in the summer of 2005 perhaps best summed up what can happen: "I can almost understand it. I can see how a young person becomes disturbed and upset and isolated, and then they become an easy target for an elder peer, which is what I suspect happened. And you turn to religion for authority. . . . They [the suicide bombers in Britain] were still trying to find a role in the world, and it was easy for them to be drawn to martyrdom. It looks like heroism, like kind of a macho, heroic act." Unfortunately, young suicide bombers don't live long enough to find out that the issues are far more complex than that.

# SOURCE NOTES

8    "Story of a Suicide Bombing," *BBC News*, http://news.bbc.co.uk/1/ hi/world/middle_east/2071403, July 18, 2002 (4/26/05).

9    Ralph Nurnberger, "How Hamas Has Attained Political Power," *Miami Herald*, January 27, 2006, 25A.

14    Christopher Reuter, *My Life Is a Weapon: A Modern History of Suicide Bombing* (Princeton, NJ: Princeton University Press, 2004), 15.

14    Barbara Victor, *Army of Roses: Inside the World of Palestinian Women Suicide Bombers* (Emmaus, PA: Rodale, 2003), 97.

15    Ibid., 39.

16–17    "CBS NEWS Interview on Suicide Bombers," October 19, 2003, *Scholar of the House*, http://www.scholarofthehouse.com/ cbsneinonsub.html (4/26/05).

17    Ibid.

20    Victor, 41.

21    Ibid., 43.

21    Ibid., 45.

24    Mia Bloom, *Dying to Kill: The Allure of Suicide Terror* (New York: Columbia University Press, 2005), 148.

26    Ibid., 19–20.

26–27    James Bennet, "The Mideast Turmoil: Killer of 3," *New York Times*, May 30, 2003, 1A.

27    Ibid.

28–29    Vered Levy-Barzilai, "Ticking Bomb," October 15, 2003, *Occupational Hazard.org*, http://www.occupationalhazard.org/ article.php?IDD=636 (4/26/2006).

29    Ibid.

30–31    Victor, p. 100.

31    Ibid., 102–103.

31    Ibid., 104.

31    Ibid., 105.

34    Lee Keath, "Female Bomber Kills Six Recruits," *The Herald*, September 29, 2005, 13A.

34    Ibid.

35–36    *Jihad Watch*, July 17, 2004, http:www.jihadwatch.org/ archives/002552.phpf (April 10, 2005).

36    Reuter, 109.

36    Jessica Stern, *Terror in the Name of God: Why Religious Militants Kill* (New York: Harper Collins, 2003), 50.

37    Joyce M. Davis, *Martyrs: Innocence, Vengeance, and Despair in the Middle East* (New York: Palgrave, 2003), 104.

37–38    Ibid., 105.

38    Aparisim Ghosh, "Inside the Mind of an Iraqi Bomber," *Time*, July 4, 2005, 26.

38    Ibid.

39    Ibid.

39–40    Ibid., 29.

41    Ibid.

41    Rod Norland, Tom Masland, and Christopher Dickey, "Unmasking the Insurgents," *Newsweek*, February 7, 2005, 29.

41    Reuter, 114.

42    Stern, 52–53.

44    Ibid., 55.

44    Sharon Begley, "Many Suicide Bombers Are Educated, Come from Well-Off Families; Little Evidence of Mental Instability," *Wall Street Journal,* October 8, 2004, B1.

44    Ibid.

45    Ellis Shuman, "What Makes Suicide Bombers Tick?" *Israel Insider*, June 4, 2001, http://www.israelinsider.com/channels/security/articles (April 10, 2005).

45    Ibid.

46    Ibid.

47    Victor, 210.

48    Davis, 137.

48    Victor, 115.

48    Stern, 59.

48–49    Ibid.

49    Reuter, 87.

50    Victor, 212.

51    Ibid., 214–215.

51    Ibid., 215.

51    Ibid.

51–52    Ibid., 217.

52    Ibid.

53    Ghosh, 26.

53    Anne Marie Oliver and Paul Steinberg, *The Road to Martyrs' Square: A Journey Into the World of the Suicide Bomber* (New York: Oxford University Press, 2005), 75.

54    Ghosh, 29.

54-55    Oliver and Steinberg, 118.

56    Ghosh, 29.

56  Ibid.

56  Oliver and Steinberg, 122.

56  Ibid.

57  Davis, 158.

58  Aparisim Ghosh, "Professor of Death," *Time*, October 24, 2005, 44–48.

58  Ibid.

58  Ibid.

58  Ibid., 129.

59  Ibid.

61  Reuter, 111.

62  Ibid.

63  Stern, 54.

63  Ibid.

63  Reuter, 112.

64  Davis, 126.

64  Barbara Victor, *An Army of Roses: Inside the World of Palestinian Women Suicide Bombers* (Emmaus, PA: Rodale Books, 2003), 261–264.

65  Davis, 135.

65  Victor, 261–264.

65  Ibid.

65  Ibid.

65  Ibid.

66  Davis, 126.

68  Ibid., 127.

68  Reuter, 110.

69  Davis, 127.

73  Edwin P. Hoyt, *The Kamikazes: Suicide Squadrons of World War II* (New York: Arbor House, 1983), 19.

74  Ibid. p. 48.

78  Ryuji Nagatsuka, *I Was a Kamikaze* (New York: Macmillan, 1972), 181.

78–80  Ibid., 188.

80–81  Ibid., 176–177.

84–85  Dean E. Murphy, *September 11: An Oral History* (New York: Doubleday, 2002), 119.

85  The Journalists of Reuters, *After September 11: New York and the World* (Upper Saddle River, NJ: Prentice Hall, 2003), 108.

86  "September 11: Chronology of Terror," *CNN.com*, September 12, 2001, http://archives.cnn.com/2001/US/09/11/chronology.attack (June 10, 2005).

86   Ibid.

88   The Reporters, Writers, and Editors of *Der Spiegel* magazine,
     *Inside 9-11: What Really Happened* (New York: St. Martin's Press,
     2001), 175.

88–89   Ibid., 183.

89   Ibid.

89   Ibid.,184.

89   Ibid., 196.

96   Mia Bloom, *Dying to Kill: The Allure of Suicide Terror* (New York:
     Columbia University Press, 2005), 130.

96   Paul Quinn-Judge, "They Are Killing Us All," *Newsweek*,
     September 13, 2004, 43.

97–98   Fred Weir, "Chechen Women Join Terror's Ranks," *Women's
     International League for Peace and Freedom*, http://www
     .peacewomen.org/news/Chechnya/newsarchive03/ranks (July 11,
     2005).

98   Michael Elliot, "Rush Hour Terror," *Time*, July 18, 2005, 30.

98   David E. Kaplan and Thomas K. Grose, "On the Terrorists' Trail,"
     *U.S. News & World Report*, July 25, 2005, 23.

99–100   Matthew Chance, "Britain's Home-Grown Terrorists," *CNN.com*,
     July 14, 2005, http://www.cnn.com/2005/WORLD/europe/07/14/
     homegrown.terror/ (4/26/2006).

102   J. F. O. McAllister, "Unraveling the Plot," *Time*, July 25, 2005, 46.

103   Souad Mekhennet and Don VanNatta, Jr., "Militant London Sheik
     Has Predicted More Terror Attacks," *New York Times*, July 22,
     2005, A8.

103   Griff White, "Suicide Bombs Kill Dozens in Afghanistan,"
     *Washington Post*, January 17, 2006, A11.

104   Alan Cowell, "Bombs Set At 4 London Sites, But Fail to
     Explode," *New York Times*, July 22, 2005, A1.

104   Bruce Hoffman, "The Logic of Suicide Terrorism," *Atlantic
     Monthly*, June 2003, 43.

105   Griff White, "Suicide Bombs Kill Dozens in Afghanistan,"
     *Washington Post*, January 17, 2006, p. A11.

107–108   Hoffman, p. 47.

108   Gregory Katz, "Britain Seeking Ways to Curb 'Evil Ideology,'"
     *Houston Chronicle*, July 17 , 2005, A1.

# SELECTED BIBLIOGRAPHY

Bloom, Mia. *Dying to Kill: The Allure of Suicide Terror*. New York: Columbia University Press, 2005.

Braiker, Harriet B. *The September 11 Syndrome: Anxious Days and Sleepless Nights*. New York: McGraw-Hill, 2002.

Clarke, Richard A. *Against All Enemies: Inside America's War on Terror*. New York: Free Press, 2004.

Davis, Joyce M. *Martyrs: Innocence, Vengeance, and Despair in the Middle East*. New York: Palgrave, 2003.

Emerson, Steven. *American Jihad: The Terrorists Living Among Us*. New York: Free Press, 2002.

Gertz, Bill. *Breakdown: How America's Intelligence Failures Led to September 11*. Washington, DC: Regnery, 2002.

Halliday, Fred. *Two Hours That Shook the World: September 11, 2001: Causes & Consequences*. London: Saqi Books, 2002.

Hoyt, Edwin P. *The Kamikazes: Suicide Squadrons of World War II*. New York: Arbor House, 1983.

Inoguchi, Rikihei, Tadashi Nakajima, and Roger Pineau. *The Divine Wind: Japan's Kamikaze Force in World War II*. Annapolis, MD: United States Naval Institute, 1958.

The Journalists of Reuters. *After September 11: New York and the World*. Upper Saddle River, NJ: Prentice Hall, 2003.

Murphy, Dean E. *September 11: An Oral History*. New York: Doubleday, 2002.

Nagatsuka, Ryuji. *I Was a Kamikaze*. New York: Macmillan, 1972.

Oliver, Anne Marie, and Paul Steinberg. *The Road to Martyrs' Square: A Journey Into the World of the Suicide Bomber*. New York: Oxford University Press, 2005.

Page, Robert. *Dying to Win: The Logic of Suicide Terrorism*. New York: Random House, 2005.

The Reporters, Writers, and Editors of *Der Spiegel Magazine*. *Inside 9-11: What Really Happened*. New York: St. Martin's Press, 2001.

Reuter, Christopher. *My Life Is a Weapon: A Modern History of Suicide Bombing*. Princeton, NJ: Princeton University Press, 2004.

Rubenberg, Cheryl A. *The Palestinians: In Search of a Just Peace*. Boulder, CO: Lynne Rienner Publishers, 2003.

Stern, Jessica. *Terror in the Name of God: Why Religious Militants Kill*. New York: HarperCollins, 2003.

Victor, Barbara. *Army of Roses: Inside the World of Palestinian Women Suicide Bombers*. Emmaus, PA: Rodale, 2003.

# Further Reading and Websites

Andryszewski, Tricia. *Terrorism in America*. Brookfield, CT: Millbrook Press, 2002.

Currie, Stephen. *Terrorists and Terrorist Groups*. San Diego, CA: Lucent Books, 2002.

Frank, Mitchell. *Understanding September 11th: Answering Questions about Attacks on America*. New York: Viking, 2002.

Fridell, Ron. *Terrorism: Political Violence at Home and Abroad*. Berkeley Heights, NJ: Enslow Publishers, 2001.

Friedman, Lauri S. *What Motivates Suicide Bombers?* San Diego: Greenhaven Press, 2004.

Gay, Kathlyn. *Silent Death: The Threat of Biological and Chemical Terrorism*. Brookfield, CT: Twenty-First Century Books, 2001.

Gow, Mary. *Attack on America: The Day the Twin Towers Collapsed*. Berkeley Heights, NJ: Enslow Publishers, 2002.

Katz, Samuel M. *Against All Odds: Counterterrorist Hostage Rescues*. Minneapolis: Lerner Publications, 2005.

———. *At Any Cost: National Liberation Terrorism*. Minneapolis: Lerner Publications, 2003.

———. *Global Counterstrike: International Counterterrorism*. Minneapolis: Lerner Publications, 2005.

———. *Jerusalem or Death: Palestinian Terrorism*. Minneapolis: Lerner Publications, 2003.

———. *Jihad: Islamic Fundamentalist Terrorism*. Minneapolis: Lerner Publications, 2003.

———. *Raging Within: Ideological Terrorism*. Minneapolis: Lerner Publications, 2003.

———. *Targeting Terror: Counterterrorist Raids*. Minneapolis: Lerner Publications, 2005.

Katz, Samuel M. *U.S. Counterstrike: American Counterterrorism*. Minneapolis: Lerner Publications, 2005.

Landau, Elaine. *Osama bin Laden: A War Against the West*. Brookfield, CT: Lerner Publishing Group, 2002.

Marcovitz, Hal. *Terrorism*. Philadelphia: Chelsea House, 2001.

Perl, Lila. *Terrorism*. Tarrytown, NY: Benchmark Books, 2004.

Stewart, Gail. *America Under Attack: September 11, 2001*. San Diego: Lucent Books, 2002.

Woolf, Alex. *Osama bin Laden*. Minneapolis: Twenty-First Century Books, 2004.

## Websites

*The War On Terrorism*—CIA

www.cia.gov/terrorism

This official CIA website offers information on various aspects of terrorism. The site has an especially interesting and informative Frequently Asked Questions section.

*Ready.gov—U.S. Department of Homeland Security*

www.ready.gov

Emergency preparedness guidance from the U.S. Department of Homeland Security.

*UN Action Against Terrorism*

www.un.org/terrorism

This website presents the latest steps taken by the United Nations to stop terrorism.

Page numbers in *italics* refer to photographs.

# About the Author

Award-winning children's book author Elaine Landau worked as a newspaper reporter, a children's book editor, and a youth services librarian before becoming a full-time writer. She has written over 250 books for young readers. Landau has a bachelor's degree in English and Journalism from New York University and a master's degree in Library and Information Science from Pratt Institute. She lives in Miami, Florida, with her husband and son. You can visit Elaine Landau at her website: www.elainelandau.com.

# Photo Acknowledgments

Photographs in this book are used with the permission of: Ohayon Avi/State of Israel National Photo Collection, pp. 6, 6–7 (background); Photo by Hamas/ZUMA Press. © 2002 by Hamas, p. 8; AP/Wide World Photos, pp. 11, 15, 22, 28, 66, 67, 75, 87, 94, 94–95 (background), 97; Milner Moshe/State of Israel National Photo Collection, pp. 18, 18–19 (background); © Getty Images, p. 25, 30; © Jerry Lampen/Reuters/Landov, p. 40; © Damir Sagolj/Reuters/Corbis, p. 43; © Jaafar Ashtiyeh/ AFP/Getty Images, p. 55; © Quique Kierszenbaum/Getty Images, pp. 60, 60–61 (background); © Keystone/Getty Images, pp. 70, 70–71 (background); © Carl Mydans/Time Life Pictures/Getty Images, p. 79; © Spencer Platt/Getty Images, pp. 82, 82–83 (background); © U.S. Navy/Getty Images, p. 90; © FBI/Getty Images, p. 91; © Plymouth County Jail/Getty Images, p. 93; © Metropolitan Police/Getty Images, p. 99; © David Silverman/Getty Images, pp. 106, 106–107 (background). Cover image by © Abid Katib/Getty Images.

5842 1017